I0881569

CLIMBING TOUBKAL

CLIMBING MOROCCO'S JEBEL TOUBKAL IN SUMMER AND WINTER – HIKING THE TOUBKAL CIRCUIT

By Emily Woodhouse

CICERONE

JUNIPER HOUSE, MURLEY MOSS,
OXENHOLME ROAD, KENDAL, CUMBRIA LA9 7RL
www.cicerone.co.uk

First edition 2025
ISBN: 978 1 78631 199 3
eISBN: 978 178765 200 2

Cicerone's EU representative for GPSR compliance is Easy Access System Europe, Mustamäe tee 50, 10621 Tallinn, Estonia. Email gpsr.requests@easproject.com.

Printed in Czechia on responsibly sourced paper on behalf of Latitude Press Ltd.

A catalogue record for this book is available from the British Library.
All photographs are by the author unless otherwise stated.
Route mapping by Oxford Alpine Club www.oxfordalpineclub.co.uk

Updates to this guide

While every effort is made by our authors to ensure the accuracy of guidebooks as they go to print, changes can occur during the lifetime of an edition. Any updates that we know of for this guide will be on the Cicerone website (www.cicerone.co.uk/1199/updates), so please check before planning your trip. We also advise that you check information about such things as transport, accommodation and shops locally. Even rights of way can be altered over time. We are always grateful for information about any discrepancies between a guidebook and the facts on the ground, sent by email to updates@cicerone.co.uk.

Register your book: To sign up to receive free updates, special offers and GPX files where available, create a Cicerone account and register your purchase via the 'My Account' tab at www.cicerone.co.uk.

Front cover: Descending the ridge from Toubkal's summit towards Tizi n'Toubkal (Route 2)

CONTENTS

Acknowledgements

Although only one person writes it, many people make a guidebook. I'd like to thank Andy Hodges – for organising the trip that finally got me to Morocco – plus Steve Ayres, Andy Wrayford, Alan Packwood and Adam Jordan for being excellent company. Adam, I'm fairly certain at least one of your photobombs made it into the book. Also, to Laura Renshaw, Jo Milner, Alex Roddie and Rosie Matthews-Brown for signing up to a trekking adventure without knowing each other beforehand and having fun in the face of a lot of unknowns. (Ellie, you were there in spirit.) Special mention to Albino Steve, the mule, and Piper, the freelance mountain dog. To all our local guides, who not only led the way but who were also our connection with their culture and community – especially Faiçal Bourkiba, who is so passionate about spreading the good news of mountaineering in Morocco. And to Alice Morrison and her world-famous cakes.

Symbols used on route maps

route	campsite
alternative route	accommodation
start point	refuge
finish point	key landmark
start/finish point	viewpoint
route direction	refreshments
peak	grocery store
footbridge	route option
road bridge	
pass	
waterfall	
water feature	
other feature	

All map measurements are in metres.

SCALE: 1:25,000

0 kilometres 0.25 0.5
0 miles 0.25

Contour lines are drawn at 25m intervals and highlighted at 100m intervals.

SCALE: 1:50,000

0 kilometres 0.5 1
0 miles 0.5

Contour lines are drawn at 25m intervals and highlighted at 100m intervals.

GPX files for all routes can be downloaded free at www.cicerone.co.uk/1199/GPX.

Helicopter rescue

The following signals are used to communicate with a helicopter:

Help needed
Raise both arms above head to form a 'Y'

Help not needed
Raise one arm above head and extend the other downward, to form the diagonal of an 'N'

Setting out from Tacheddirt towards the distant pass on the horizon (Toubkal Circuit, Stage 2)

ROUTE SUMMARY TABLES

Route	Walk title	Start/Finish	Distance (km)	Ascent (m)	Descent (m)	Time	Page
Winter							
1	Imlil to Base Camp	Toubkal trailhead/ Base Camp	8	1300	0	5hr+	60
2	Base Camp to Toubkal summit – Ikhibi Sud	Base Camp	3	1000	1000	6hr	65
3	Base Camp to Toubkal summit – Ikhibi Nord	Base Camp	4	1100	1100	7hr	69
4	Aougdal Bou Tioana gully	Base Camp	3.5	500	500	3hr	72
5	Tizi n'Ouanoums	Base Camp	2	500	500	3hr	75
6	Ouanoukrim	Base Camp	8	1000	1000	6hr+	78
Summer							
7	Imlil Cascades	Imlil's main car park	3	300	300	1hr	88
8	Imlil to Base Camp	Toubkal trailhead/ Base Camp	9	1300	0	4½–5hr	92
9	Base Camp to Toubkal summit – Ikhibi Sud	Base Camp	3.5	1100	1100	6hr	97
10	Base Camp to Toubkal summit – Ikhibi Nord	Base Camp	4	1100	1100	7hr	101
11	Full Toubkal Horseshoe	Base Camp	9	1300	1300	7–8hr	105
12	Ouanoukrim	Base Camp	8.5	1100	1100	6–7hr	108
13	Aguelzim	Base Camp	9	1000	1000	4–5hr	115

On Ouanoukrim's scramble ridge (Route 12)

TOUBKAL CIRCUIT

Stage	Start	Finish	Distance (km)	Ascent (m)	Descent (m)	Time	Page
1	Imlil	Tacheddirt	11.5	1050	400	4–5hr	121
2	Tacheddirt	Azib Likemt	11.5	1250	1100	6–7hr	125
3	Azib Likemt	Amsouzert	15.5	850	1650	7–8hr	129
4	Amsouzert	Lake Ifni	9.5	1000	450	5hr	134
5	Lake Ifni	Toubkal Base Camp	9	1550	700	7–8hr	137
6	Toubkal Base Camp	Imlil	10.5	150	1550	3–4hr	142
		Total	**67.5**	**5850**	**5850**	**32hr**	

Setting out from Base Camp at sunrise (Route 2)

INTRODUCTION

Taking in the view of Toubkal and Dome d'Ifni from Ras (Route 12)

Sitting in an air-conditioned mini-van, driving away from Marrakech, I stared out of the window. Speeding along the perfectly straight road, the landscape whipping past: dirt-red walls, back-of-a-truck fruit stalls, uniform rows of wrinkled olive trees. As I looked up, my gaze settled on a band of cloud in the distance, a line of white that hovered in a long, straight strip above the horizon. Then suddenly it wasn't cloud: it was a range of mountains.

I remember that moment vividly; it was like the mountains had pulled a magic trick on me. For all the hours I'd spent idly imagining mountains in the clouds, there was nothing like the surprise of realising that those clouds were in fact mountains. The Jbel Toubkal end of the High Atlas mountain range spreads out across the horizon on the drive south from Marrakech, visible through the haze when cloaked in its winter white and a fitting view for the start of any Moroccan mountain adventure.

In recent years, more and more people have looked to Morocco for hiking, trekking and mountaineering, with Jbel Toubkal (4167m), the highest peak in North Africa, the main allure. Its distinctive black metal summit pyramid has formed the background to many a group photo: the people clustered in front – exhausted, elated, relieved – grinning into the camera in snow or shine. Sometimes both.

I first heard of Toubkal when I was working in the adventure travel industry. It was being sold as a mini-Kilimanjaro: shorter in height, shorter in distance, with all the excitement and culture of Africa – albeit a very different Africa to Tanzania. When I eventually came, it was for the winter mountaineering because the mountains looked more interesting and exploratory than anything the Alps could offer. I was captured by the newness of it all: the relative lack of infrastructure, systems and standards. It felt like being on the cusp of something great – with the attention growing and everything on the ground accelerating to catch up. But I was also very aware that hikers were coming from around the world, ready or not.

The one person not credited in the acknowledgements, who probably should be, is the lady who fell unconscious at our feet halfway up Toubkal. You do not have to be the world's most experienced first-aider to help save a life. Nor do you need to be the most experienced mountaineer to write a guidebook for beginners. Along with other incidents witnessed on our trip, it made me realise that I really wanted to help. It felt like there was a real need for a detailed, up-to-date English language guidebook to help cut through the confusion and misinformation online – never mind the marketing hyperbole.

Maybe you've been brought here by that – by stories of challenging but rewarding ascents, sunrise summits and views over the Sahara. There is a lot of truth in it. The mountains of Toubkal National Park are some of my favourites in the world, and not just because I've spent the past two years immersed in their trails, maps and history in researching this book. They are also home to the Toubkal Circuit trekking route, arguably one of the best multi-day treks in Africa.

So, you're thinking about Toubkal? Great. I'm here to lead you beyond the idea and through the practical process of choosing, designing and preparing for your trip step by step. And to take you through some options route by route. There is so much more to these mountains than Jbel Toubkal if you have the time and sense of adventure required to step off the common path. So, without further ado, let's begin.

View towards Lake Ifni, seen in the distance (Route 5)

TRAVEL – YOUR JOURNEY TO TOUBKAL

Morocco has four main mountain ranges: the High Atlas, the Middle Atlas, the Anti-Atlas and the Rif mountains. Its capital city is Rabat. Along with Fez, Marrakesh and Meknes, it makes up the four Imperial Cities of Morocco – all capitals at some point in the country's history. The largest city is Casablanca, on the coast, and Tangier is another large port city, close to Spain.

The key points in your journey to the foot of Toubkal are Marrakech and Imlil. Marrakech is an ancient walled city, the closest city to the High Atlas and where many people's journey through Morocco begins. Imlil is a growing mountain village at the start of the main trail to Toubkal.

Marrakech

Founded in the 11th century, the old city of Marrakech, the medina, is contained within 19km of high, earth-red defensive walls, but modern Marrakech spills out far beyond into the surrounding plains. For tourists, the city is most famous for its markets and souks: winding mazes of covered streets where each alcove is filled with wares – stalls selling carpets, jewellery, spices, tagines and ceramics, lamps, teapots and leather. The most famous (notorious) square is Jemaa el-Fnaa within the medina. During the day there are souvenir stalls, juice stands and snake charmers. At night, it fills with street food, storytellers, performers and even more people. It is not a calm shopping experience. Hotels, riads, hostels, cafés, restaurants, shops, supermarkets, banks, ATMs (including at Marrakech airport), tourist information, buses, taxis, and an airport are all available in Marrakech.

Other tourist destinations and activities include walking the many

Marrakech

gardens; visiting mosques, palaces and museums; or taking a hammam (the Moroccan version of a Turkish bath). If it's not too hot, visitors also enjoy walking along the outside of the ramparts as a way to explore. Unfortunately, you can't get up on top of the walls for a view.

Many visiting the High Atlas will spend a night in Marrakech, at one or both ends of their journey, but don't feel that you have to. It is a very busy city and a huge culture shock compared with the peace of the mountains, although it does add an extra cultural and historical perspective to the Moroccan experience. The medina was designated a UNESCO World Heritage Site in 1985.

Travel to Morocco

How to get to Morocco? It really depends upon your starting point, but most international visitors will fly. Marrakech (RAK) is the closest airport to Toubkal and has direct flight connections with the UK, the US, Canada and many airports in Europe. For more options from the US and Canada, plus direct flights from the Middle East, Casablanca airport is an alternative. Flights from the UK and Western Europe are only 3–4hr long, making it a fairly short flight despite it being North Africa. This has led to a boom in popularity with tourists. Check for the most up-to-date information, as more direct flight routes are constantly being added. Also, allow plenty of time in your travel schedule for negotiating the airport (both ways), as Marrakech is notoriously slow – especially in summer.

Given Morocco's close proximity to Spain, separated by only about 15 miles of sea across the Strait of Gibraltar, it is possible to travel overland from Europe. Using the high-speed rail service that connects major European cities, you can reach either Algeciras or Tarifa at the southern tip of Spain. Both these ferries dock at Tangier and the corssing takes about 2½hr.

To reach Marrakech from Tangier or Casablanca, you can take a direct train. Alternatively, the CTM or Supratours buses make for a comfortable journey, if long. Tickets can be bought online from the respective companies' websites or at the bus station.

Marrakech airport makes a simple and well-connected meeting point if you are bypassing the city and heading straight to the mountains.

Visas and permits

For many citizenships – including UK, US, Canada, Australia, New Zealand, Japan and most European Union countries – there is no need to apply for a tourist visa if your stay is up to a maximum of 90 days. You can check the most up-to-date requirements via your country's Foreign Office or contact the Moroccan Ministry of Foreign Affairs, consulat.ma. For those used to visiting wilderness areas requiring permits, it's worth mentioning here that no permits are required for Toubkal National Park, although there are restrictions on how you can access the park. (See later 'Guides' section.)

Transport within Morocco

There is no direct bus connection to Imlil from Marrakech, so you will need to arrange some sort of taxi transport to reach the mountains. Car hire is possible but unnecessary if you intend to travel mostly on foot. It also saddles you with a parked car that needs to be returned to and thought about. It is possible to get a bus from Marrakech to Asni and then change onto a green minibus for the last section to Imlil. Local bus travel can be a whole adventure in itself for the unsuspecting tourist, so it's far simpler to book a taxi. In Morocco there are two types of taxi: *petit* (small) and *grand* (large).

Grand taxis are six-seater vehicles that operate shared transport between a city and the nearby towns and villages where no bus route exists. These can be notoriously cramped but do allow the solo traveller to reach Imlil. Alternatively, shared minibuses also run between Marrakech and Asni.

Petit taxis are smaller, shared vehicles that operate only within cities. You cannot take one to Imlil. They take a maximum of three passengers and use a meter. If there is no meter or if it is broken, make sure you agree a price before you get in. Taxi ranks can be found in the main tourist areas, including Marrakech airport, but you can also hail them in the street.

If you are spending a night in Marrakech, your hotel will be able to suggest some transfer options from Marrakech to Imlil. The trip takes roughly 1½hr. Make sure to bring plenty of water for this journey, especially in summer, as you might not be able to stop to buy or fill up on water on the way. (This might mean refilling your bottle after passing through security in your home-country airport, as

Asni

there are currently no water fountains at Marrakech airport.)

To avoid any hassle at the start of your trip, many local guides will simply book transport for you and lump it into their fee. Similarly, if you are using a package holiday company or joining a tour group, they will be able to suggest transport providers to Imlil – or quite probably arrange it for you. Make sure to check all your inclusions ahead of time.

If you are travelling as an independent group, booking out a private taxi instead of using public transport has its benefits: the main one being the freedom to stop where and when you please. On the way from Marrakech to Imlil, many people break the journey at Asni for lunch or a leg stretch.

Asni

Asni is a small town, the last one you pass through on the way to Imlil. It is mostly known for its weekly markets, where people from villages all around come to buy food and other goods. Walking through a market, you'll see fruit and vegetables arranged on low tables or laid out on carpets. Sometimes there is second-hand outdoor gear. The main high street has many café-restaurants and amenities. Notably, this is your last chance to access an ATM before Toubkal. Be careful: cash can run out on market days. Riads, a hostel, cafés, restaurants, a bakery, a pharmacy, a bank (with an ATM) and a weekly market on Saturdays are all available.

Imlil

Imlil is the principal village at the foot of the valley below Toubkal and the main access point for most people attempting to summit. The trail between Imlil and Toubkal, via Toubkal Base Camp, is the shortest possible distance. Imlil has a large car park, on the left of the road as you approach, and a small high street containing most of the shops. Depending on the time of year, you'll walk past shop fronts hung with rows of trekking poles, crampons and old rucksacks, as well as all sorts of second-hand gear for sale. You'll find freshly pressed peanut butter, cafés with seating areas under the shade of walnut trees and carpet co-operatives with bright woven rugs displayed over every surface to entice customers inside. You can also buy novelty 'I Climbed Toubkal' T-shirts and a small amount of other memorabilia. Make sure you have dirham as most of the shops here will not accept any other currency. A hotel, riads, gîtes, a youth hostel, cafés, restaurants, shops, a bakery, a pharmacy, outdoor gear and taxis are available.

Aremd

Like most of the High Atlas valleys, there are several small villages or hamlets spread throughout the Imlil valley. Aremd (pronounced 'R-med', also spelt variously Aroumd, Armed, Around) is a large settlement on the hillside at the top of the Imlil valley, right by the starting point for the Toubkal Trail. There was an alpine hut here sometime in the 1920s–30s, before Imlil grew. During the summer, the waterfall between Imlil and Aremd is a popular day trip for Moroccans and tourists alike.

ACCOMMODATION

Plenty of accommodation options are available at all stages of your journey. For either end of your adventure and during the trek, here are the types of accommodation you may encounter.

Imlil

Imlil town map
car park and
taxi rank
Ait Souka
Bureau
des Guides
gift shops
Imlil Cascades
N
0
300
m
Aremd
police checkpoint
in winter
Toubkal trailhead
Toubkal trailhead

1 **Riad** – a riad is a townhouse: a tall, usually terraced, building with many small private rooms over several floors, characterised by its central courtyard garden with a fountain and tables to sit at. This is not an enclosed courtyard surrounded by windows but more of a central living area with an open roof and a clear view up to the sky. You can usually access the rooftop as well, for views out over the city. These beautiful houses are hidden from the outside, especially in Marrakech; they may look like just a door down a back alley. You may also come across a *dar* (a smaller version of a riad): a house over a couple of floors without the central courtyard, more like a guest house. Both function like small hotels and will provide bedding and towels.

2 **Gîte** – in Morocco, a gîte is a cross between a guest house and a hostel. Generally, they are more basic and rustic than a dar or a riad and may be either booked in their entirety or on a per-room basis. A small amount of bedding is provided.

3 **Auberge** – again from the French, an auberge is a hostel of sorts. Usually, in this part of Morocco they will have shared rooms and shared bathrooms. In small mountain villages, you might have four single beds to a room. A basic bedding set of sheet, blanket and pillow is provided.

4 **Hotels** – for completeness, you can also stay in modern hotels in Marrakech. Even five-star accommodation is available in the vicinity of Imlil.

A riad in Marrakech

When booking accommodation for before or after your hike, you need to take a few things into consideration. Firstly, are the bathrooms private or shared? Unfortunately, private bathrooms are not always cleaner. If they are shared, how many are there? Some hostels in Marrakech have only one bathroom for the entire building. Next, in summer, do the rooms have air conditioning? This is less of an issue when you are in the mountains, where temperatures are cooler, but when it's 37°C in Marrakech you might be glad of it. Similarly, you cannot assume that the tap water is drinkable, even in Marrakech. Also, check whether it is possible to dine at your accommodation or whether you'll need to venture out into the town or city. Finally, read the online one-star reviews – especially in Marrakech, where you are overwhelmed by the choice of accommodation. Your experience will (hopefully!) be a lot better, but they can be very revealing and help you to prepare for the worst possibilities.

As for deep inside Toubkal National Park, you have the option of camping or, while at Toubkal Base Camp, staying in one of the two refuges. In both cases, the dormitories have alpine bunks.

Les Mouflons

Les Mouflons Toubkal is an independently owned refuge built by a local entrepreneur and opened in 2007. It has capacity for 180 people across a number of large, shared dorms and private rooms. This is the first refuge you come to when ascending from Imlil. It has a spacious, enclosed foyer for de-kitting in winter, with steps downstairs to the kitchen (no public access). Inside there are two dining/living areas downstairs, a reception and shop, shared showers and toilets. Upstairs are bedrooms, more toilets and access onto a balcony. Two large fireplaces downstairs provide heating in the winter. The refuge is large and spacious with a clear Moroccan influence in its décor. It is quite dark and the open-plan design means the rooms do get cold in winter.

- 2 showers
- 4 toilets
- Shop with snacks and bottled water
- Limited electricity
- Meals usually provided independent of refuge
- Camping options in summer
- See refugetoubkal.com

CAF Toubkal

The CAF Toubkal refuge is owned by the Club Alpin Français (French Alpine Club), who have had a building on the site since 1939. Built in 1999, the current refuge replaced the smaller Neltner refuge, now disused. It has a capacity of 86 people across 4 large dormitories. The living space is much smaller than Les Mouflons next door, with a dining room and two living rooms, including a log-burning stove. The bathrooms are downstairs,

The CAF Toubkal refuge with Les Mouflons behind (above) and Les Mouflons refuge (below)

including the showers and toilets, and the bedrooms are upstairs. It has some of the feel of an alpine hut and is bright and comfortable despite its smaller size and small windows.

- 2 showers
- 4 toilets
- Boot room
- Electricity
- Café
- Wi-Fi (not fast!)
- Meals usually provided by refuge
- See refugedutoubkal.com

You may still see references to the Neltner refuge online and on maps. Although the building is physically still there, it is now used as an animal shelter and cannot be slept in. This was the first CAF refuge in the area – see 'A history of mountaineering in Morocco' for more detail.

Camping

At Toubkal Base Camp there is camping space on the grassy terraces in front of the Les Mouflons refuge in summer. On treks, camps are set up at specific, approved locations but there are generally no facilities. Tents are usually provided and pitched in advance of your arrival; these are normally two-person tents and can be anything from modern to battered. You will also have a large cook tent, which will be used as a living space, kitchen and dining room. Your guide and any other trekking support staff will sleep in this tent too. Depending on the campsite, they may use pre-existing shelters rather than pitch the big tent, if it's more comfortable.

GUIDES

Do I need a guide? The short answer is yes. In December 2018, two Scandinavian backpackers, university students in Norway, were brutally murdered in their tents while camping in the hills above Imlil. This was shocking to the local community – nothing like it had happened before or since – and the government cracked down hard, increasing security against potential terrorists. Three police checkpoints are now located along the main Toubkal Trail from Imlil: one at the trail head, one halfway and another at Base Camp. It is possible that only the bottom checkpoint will be open in winter. Note that they will not let you pass without a guide.

Since this incident, it is mandatory for visitors to take a guide while hiking within Toubkal National Park. This is not something you can avoid. Even if the police checkpoints are shut, or you think you can sneak past, it will be obvious that you are the only group without a local guide. Everyone knows everyone on the mountain, and you will not be allowed to stay at either of the Toubkal refuges, or camp nearby, without declaring who your guide is when booking or on arrival. This may feel particularly unfair if you hold mountain leader/guide qualifications that are likely to be higher than your local guide's. But at present there is no way around this. International mountain qualifications are not recognised.

In terms of qualifications, a good local guide will have plenty of experience in the high peaks of the national park. There is a diploma is offered in Morocco, at the Centre de Formation aux Métiers de la Montagne (CFMM), at Tabant, in the Ait Bougmez valley below M'Goun. It is not clear what is involved in the six months' training, but the application for the programme is very competitive. Some guides do extra training in France. Even though qualifications do exist, they are far from mandatory and you will encounter many people selling guiding services without them. A licensed guide is one who has been officially approved by the authorities: passing an interview and a small city-based fitness test. The licensing process is not specific to the mountains.

What to expect from a guide? As in all countries worldwide, not all guides are made equal. Some will have higher qualifications than others. Some will have many years of experience and others will be new to the job. Although the Imlil Guides Office is often presented as the place to go for the best local guides – with some 60 on their roster – looking at recent reviews, there is still a long way to go. Many other good, independent guides and providers exist. Do not expect the kind of attentive, group-forming service one takes as standard in the Western world. Most guides do literally that: guide the way. It is up to you to say if you need to stop on a long ascent or if you want to wait for the back of the group to catch up. Similarly, tensions can arise if your group is very experienced in mountain environments (particularly winter conditions) and your guide is not. Choose well and wisely.

Guides are more likely to speak French than English, but neither language is a given. Arabic is the most spoken language, with a Moroccan dialect. Although good outdoor equipment is becoming more readily available in Morocco, guides will not

The path to Sidi Chamharouch winds around the valley's slopes (Route 8)

be wearing fancy alpine kit. However, you can still, in some respects, judge the preparedness of a guide by the size of his rucksack. Note that there are very few female mountain guides in Morocco.

So, you need to find a guide and a decent one at that. But how do you possibly go about finding one? There are three main directions you can take to find a good guide.

A foreign (home country) provider

A huge variety of package tours and adventure holidays, all with the goal of climbing Toubkal, have sprung up in recent years. Some of these will use only local guides, while others will pair a local guide with a leader native to your home country, to smooth over any language or cultural differences.

Pros:

- Zero-hassle booking
- End-to-end service
- Easy to join a group as a solo traveller

Cons:

- Generally more expensive
- Less flexibility in objectives: most climb only Toubkal or perhaps Ouanoukrim too.

A small number of foreign guides living locally to Toubkal can also provide a more customised trip with many of the benefits listed above.

Local providers

A growing number of small businesses are offering tour packages within Morocco. Just as in other countries, these are generally run by a local guide with a number of employees or freelancers. They generally have websites and will respond to email enquiries. Some are listed on sites like Tripadvisor so you can see their recent reviews. Many of the foreign tour operators work with these small companies and if you are sneaky, you can work out which from their testimonials and book direct.

Pros:

- Similar to foreign providers – offering set packages – but cheaper
- Low-hassle booking
- More variety in routes and objectives

Cons:

- Can be quite rigid in price and itinerary
- Payment may be required in one lump sum for the whole group or cash on arrival

Individual guides

You can also book directly with an individual guide, who generally works for themself as well as freelancing for other companies. It is possible to pick up a guide once you arrive in Morocco, but it's advisable to book ahead if you are planning to do anything more than the standard up and down Toubkal. And besides, you'll feel more reassured of your guide's competence if you plan ahead rather than find them on the streets of Imlil. Everyone knows everyone in Morocco, and anyone you ask will try to recommend their brother/cousin/nephew, etc. It is very easy to find a guide – but it is quite hard to vet them. However, enough people have visited the High Atlas now that if you ask around at home (friends, colleagues, local mountaineering clubs, online groups, etc.) someone will know someone who can introduce you to the guide they used. Most guides use WhatsApp, so a good introduction can be made by three-way text, to make sure you get a fair price.

Pros:

- Complete flexibility in itinerary
- Cheaper

Cons:

- Huge variety in service: look for a personal recommendation
- Lots of back and forth to organise a trip

While researching and booking a guide, here are a few questions to ask. Firstly, ask for their licence number. All official guides licensed by the authorities to lead tourists in Morocco should have one. Ask how long they have been guiding and, specifically, how many times they have done the particular routes and peaks you are suggesting (note that experience in summer and winter is very different).

A large communal cook tent on the Toubkal circuit trek

Which training courses have they done? You should also check which languages they speak.

MULES, MULETEERS, PORTERS AND COOKS

As well as your guide, you may be accompanied by several other local people while in the mountains; these include cooks, muleteers and porters. Some double up on roles, but you can expect at least one or two extra people with your group, more if you are going on a long summer trek. It can feel strange to trek with such an entourage but it is the Moroccan way.

Cook

Cooks are, unsurprisingly, the people who prepare food for the group. On a trek, they will use a corner of the big tent as a kitchen, squatting in front of a pressure cooker balanced on a camping stove. At the Toubkal refuges, they will either cook outside in a tent or use the kitchen downstairs at Les Mouflons. You will be provided with three meals a day – breakfast, lunch and dinner – plus mid-afternoon tea and, if you are on a trek, possibly a small, packed lunch at the top of the day's pass.

Muleteers

In summer months, mules are used to carry excess bags, luggage, food and drinking water along suitable trails. They are particularly useful for multi-day treks, such as the Toubkal Circuit, allowing hikers to carry a small, light rucksack rather than an expedition pack. Many groups choose to use mules on the ascent from Imlil to Toubkal Base Camp. In winter, mules can be used only up to the snowline or until it becomes too icy for them to climb higher.

Muleteers are in charge of the group's mules. They walk with them, sometimes leading them, sometimes holding onto their tails to direct them along the trail. Generally, a trekking group of six people might have three mules carrying bags, but most of the load is food, tents and mattresses. Trekkers will usually set out early while the mules are still being packed. Then, at some point, the mules will overtake and arrive at the day's destination before the trekkers. At camp, mules are free to graze or are tied to a long rope. There are terraced, grassy slopes below the Toubkal refuges in summer. In winter, mules cannot access Base Camp due to snow and ice – if used for a short section from Imlil, they will be unloaded and returned to the valley.

Equipment is stored in two large, woven bags, one on each side of the mule's saddle. If you are packing extra luggage, a duffle bag or large dry bag is best. However, don't put anything too valuable or breakable into this luggage. The bags will be quite unceremoniously thrown around. If you're worried about something, carry it yourself. Even if you do not bring any extra luggage, a guide may insist on using mules to carry food and water.

ETHICS

A mule is a cross between a horse and a donkey, specially bred for carrying heavy loads. Good muleteers never overburden their mules – and it's not in their interest to do anything that might hurt the mule. A mule is very expensive and represents the owner's livelihood. As for how much weight they carry, I have heard 75kg maximum or 125–150kg, depending on who you ask. One thing you can do to reduce the burden on your mules is to pack light. This may sound obvious, but it is very common to see mules heading up the trail from Imlil to Toubkal Base Camp loaded up with 100L duffle bags, aeroplane luggage tags still attached. You do not need that much stuff!

If your mule appears to be injured, you can speak up and refuse to use it until it is treated. There is a Mules Association, who help to improve the conditions for working mules in Toubkal National Park. If you see a mule carrying a large rock in one of its bags, this is to balance out the weight from the other side – not to punish it.

Entering the woods (Toubkal Circuit, Stage 1)

Porters

In winter, snow conditions mean that mules cannot be used in the high mountains or over high passes, but all the food, drinking water and luggage must still be carried into the mountains somehow... and if you are not carrying it, someone is. There is certainly no drop-off or cable system like those used at some of the refuges in the Alps. Often, the group's cook will double as a porter. Do not be surprised if you are overtaken by a man in wellies with a 70L duffle bag slung over his shoulders! And try not to take it personally. These are very fit, well-acclimatised mountain people who earn an honest living. Kit is improving year on year, but they make do with what they have.

WHEN TO GO?

The time of year you choose to climb Toubkal will dictate the type of trip you have. In summer, Toubkal is a trekking peak. In winter, it is a serious undertaking.

The Toubkal area of the High Atlas mountains essentially has two seasons: summer and winter. Summer conditions (i.e. no, or very little, snow on the ground) start from June through to the beginning of September. Patches of snow may still be found above 3000m but all of the high passes will be snow free. Winter conditions can be expected from December through to the end of March, but snow can start to fall as early as October in some years. The snowline varies depending on the

Toubkal West (Route 2)

winter, commonly around 2000m, but snow cover may extend all the way down to the valley villages.

Of course, no two winters are the same and snowfall in the high mountains is becoming increasingly unpredictable. Some winters have good enough snow coverage for alpinism and winter mountaineering, whereas others are very dry with only a layer of ice at the summit of Toubkal. (Equally, this can vary week on week, with snowstorms coming in then melting away.) Sadly, there is no guarantee that you will get good snow conditions. This is of particular importance when booking onto commercial trips selling winter experiences at the end of the season: if you come expecting lots of snow, you may be disappointed.

Either way, you should expect to need, and certainly carry, an ice axe and crampons between December and the end of March. Conversely, you should expect hot, dry weather during June, July and August – although sudden torrential rain showers are possible from late July. During spring and autumn, the weather is variable. April and May, even the end of March some years, is the season of snow melt, with rapidly warming temperatures turning the snow to slush. On the flip side, in September, October and November, rain can turn to snow in the high mountains as the temperature cools.

There is nothing to stop you from visiting in these off-seasons, just expect variable conditions underfoot and overhead. September and October are the walnut-harvesting season, so more people in the villages will be busy with agriculture. You'll also struggle to find an early-season guide who will travel expedition style (without mules or support) on the Toubkal Circuit, and you'll have to wait until the passes are snow free in June – or maybe late May after a dry winter.

To make a very rough assessment of the temperature in the mountains,

WEATHER FORECAST

There is no dedicated mountain weather forecast for Toubkal National Park. You can check one of the many weather apps and websites available online, but forecasts are often simply wrong, even for the next day. This is especially true in terms of specifics like wind speed and direction. To get an idea of the conditions on the ground on the run-up to your trip, try contacting locals, such as your guide or your accommodation owner, and ask about the current weather conditions. Social media posts of other people's trips, or from local businesses, in the weeks and days before your trip will also give an idea of the recent conditions, especially photos taken on Toubkal summit and in Imlil.

find a forecast for Imlil (1750m) or Marrakech (500m) and reduce it by 14°C or 27°C, respectively, to arrive at an approximate temperature for Toubkal Base Camp (3200m). The rule of thumb is that you lose 1°C for every 100m of ascent, not taking into account wind chill. So, if it's 30°C in Marrakech, it'll be about 16°C in Imlil and about 4°C at Toubkal Base Camp, although it will feel warmer in the sun. And by the same rough calculation, it will be below zero on the summit of Toubkal (4167m). Adding wind chill into the equation, it could easily feel like -10°C in summer and -20°C in winter.

Another consideration when planning your trip is Ramadan: a Muslim month of fasting that moves from year to year. During this time, no food or water is consumed between dawn and dusk. In general, this can mean that cafés and restaurants are closed during the day, and banks will open late and close mid-afternoon. It is wise to look up the dates for Ramadan before planning your trip. And if you are intending to climb Toubkal during these dates, ask your guide how it might affect your trip. Typically, foreign commercial trips will run as usual, but smaller local operations may not. Understandably, it is hard enough to climb a 4000m peak – never mind without food or water.

HOW LONG DO I NEED?

Okay, so now you have a basic grasp on all the moving parts of a trip to Toubkal; the next question is how long do I need? The answer depends mostly on the time of year and your personality.

If you just want to stand on top of Toubkal, tick it off your list and return to Marrakech pronto, it is possible to climb Toubkal in a weekend: drive from Marrakech to Imlil in the morning, hike up to a refuge for the evening, get a few hours' sleep, set out at 4am, summit for sunrise and descend

The first time I visited Toubkal, it was early March and we had climbed up from Imlil in a blizzard. Sitting in the dining room of Les Mouflons, we had just dealt out the pack of cards when everything happened at once. On the table next to us someone nearly fainted. Someone in the far corner threw up. Another man, still wearing just the waterproof and base layer he'd climbed in, was sitting alone on the end of the bench by the fire, staring into the distance and silently shivering. It was certainly a formative first impression. As it happened, all of our group were in Mountain Rescue in the UK, so we immediately tried to help. As we did, our guide said, 'Don't worry, this is normal.' People were still arriving at the front door in ones and twos past 7pm, well into the darkness and in an ongoing snowstorm. There is no reason for this to be normal.

Approaching the refuges as they appear out of the mist (Route 1)

straight back to Imlil for a taxi back to Marrakech. Possible? Certainly. Recommended? Absolutely not. We'll talk in more detail about altitude soon, but going from sea level to 4167m so quickly is a recipe for disaster, unless you happen to live at altitude. People get away with it regularly, but it makes for a fairly miserable flash in the pan. I would be highly suspicious of any operator advertising 'Climb Toubkal in a Weekend' (2 days). Do not think that just because people are selling it as a two-day trip that that makes it alright.

To climb Toubkal, with no other peaks, three to four days is a reasonable, quick schedule in summer or winter.

3 Day itinerary:

- Day 1: Marrakech to Imlil – sleep at Imlil (1750m)
- Day 2: Hike from Imlil to Base Camp – sleep at Base Camp (3200m)
- Day 3: Base Camp to summit to Imlil (and stay overnight or return to Marrakech)

4 Day itinerary:

- Day 1: Marrakech to Imlil
- Day 2: Imlil to Base Camp
- Day 3: Acclimatisation hike from Base Camp
- Day 4: Base Camp to summit to Imlil

In winter, day three of the four-day itinerary is often used to check crampon- and ice-axe skills. Many commercial trips sell this as an 'Introduction to Winter Mountaineering' course. Having an extra day in the programme allows you to see more than just Toubkal and adds a buffer day in case of bad weather or mishap.

If you want to take in extra peaks (Ouanoukrim, the second-highest peak after Toubkal, is a common extra objective), plan on four or five days.

4 Day itinerary for 2 peaks:

- Day 1: Marrakech to Imlil
- Day 2: Imlil to Base Camp
- Day 3: Base Camp to Toubkal summit to Base Camp
- Day 4: Base Camp to Ouanoukrim summit to Imlil

5 Day itinerary for 2 peaks:

- Day 1: Marrakech to Imlil
- Day 2: Imlil to Base Camp
- Day 3: Acclimatisation hike from Base Camp
- Day 4: Base Camp to Toubkal summit to Base Camp
- Day 5: Base Camp to Ouanoukrim summit to Imlil

Again, the longer itinerary adds extra flexibility. You could swap your two summit days depending on the weather. If you only have two good-weather days, you could even take out the acclimatisation hike and climb Ouanoukrim first. On the other hand, if high winds keep you at Base Camp for two days, then you'll at least still get one peak on your singular good-weather day. Meanwhile people on a three-day trip will leave empty handed. Or if a snowstorm is blowing through and you can't climb from Imlil to Base Camp until day three of your five-day trip, again, you'll at least have a chance to summit one peak. If you have the time, a longer trip is always better – especially in winter.

For even longer trips, you can design your itinerary however you like! Just remember that a slow ascent is better to avoid altitude sickness. And having a buffer of a few spare days is especially useful in winter or in the off season, to allow time for poor weather to pass through. It is okay if you don't have spare days, but just be prepared that you might not achieve everything you hope for.

Stopping for tea at the highest café (Route 1)

HEALTH AND HYGIENE

When travelling to Morocco, the recommended vaccines are for hepatitis A, hepatitis B and tetanus. Hepatitis A is a liver infection caused by a virus that spreads through contaminated faeces. Hepatitis B is also an infection of the liver but it is caused by a virus that is spread through infected blood. Tetanus is a serious infection that affects the nerves, caused when bacteria enters a cut or wound. In the UK, the NHS offers clear, comprehensive and concise guidance on Fit for Travel, see fitfortravel.nhs.uk. Check your own country's health service for the most up-to-date travel advice.

For those travelling from mainland Europe and the UK, Morocco is not covered by the EHIC (European Health Insurance Card) nor the UK's GHIC (Global Health Insurance Card). For other citizenships, check what your health insurance covers and consider taking out specialist travel insurance as you see fit. Adventure sports and high altitude may fall outside the standard cover.

When staying in accommodation – especially shared rooms with a high turnover, such as the refuges and auberges – know that it's unlikely the bedding is washed very often. Even if you don't have a sleeping bag, bringing a sheet or sheet sleeping bag will help separate your skin from shared bedding and reduce the risk of skin complaints.

Stopping for a rest at the viewpoint (Route 13)

Washing

It is possible to stay fairly clean while hiking in the Toubkal area. Accommodation in the villages will have showers, and there are showers at both Toubkal refuges, but there is no guarantee they will be warm. Remember that this water is not drinking water – so be careful not to swallow any.

For multi-day trekkers, a common trick is to wash your clothes by getting into the shower wearing them. It's considered inappropriate to hang your underwear out to dry, but you can probably find somewhere to dry the rest in summer. And if you can't wash them, don't worry. There will be plenty of people going full dirtbag, neither washing themselves nor their clothes for the duration of the trip – and that is okay. You might like to bring wet wipes for basic cleanliness and to get some of the suncream or dirt off your face – a true relief after a few sticky days. Also, make sure to bring hand sanitiser or wet wipes for the many occasions when you cannot wash your hands before a meal.

Toilets

Although there are no public toilets in Imlil or the surrounding villages, all guest accommodation will, of course, have toilets. If you were extremely desperate and not booked in anywhere overnight, you could ask at a café for help. There is at least one toilet along the main trail between Imlil and Base Camp, at Sidi Chamharouch. There are toilets at both of the Toubkal refuges but none at any higher elevation. Where toilets are not available, you will have to hold it in or squat somewhere out of sight and off the trail. (The latter is easier said than done in the most popular areas.)

On the Toubkal Circuit trek, you are never more than two days from a proper toilet. Some trekking providers will dig toilet pits at camp – affectionately known as 'long drops' – with a tall, narrow tent over the top for privacy. But this is not always possible due to the rocky ground of some locations. As these treks become more popular, toilet waste will quickly become a problem if it is not thought about soon.

While walking along quiet trails during the day, it is perfectly acceptable to drop back and hide behind a suitable rock or bush. Just make sure you tell someone in the group where you're going. Given Muslim attitudes to women showing too much skin, a common question is whether stopping like this is a problem for women, culturally. It is no problem at all, just make sure you are actually out of sight.

What to expect

You will encounter two types of toilets. The western toilet is a standard flushing toilet that you can sit down on. However, in most places in the mountains you should not flush toilet paper down the toilet. This is generally indicated by a small, open-topped dustbin next to the toilet. Inevitably, if enough people forget to use the bin, the pipes will become blocked, causing the toilet to overflow. (I have seen this happen more than once in Les Mouflons.) Obviously, nothing else manufactured should be flushed down these toilets either. Wrap it up and use the bin.

The other, arguably more common, type of toilet is the Moroccan squat toilet. This is a simple ceramic square in the floor with a hole in the middle. Instead of sitting, you are supposed to place your feet on the two anti-slip plates and squat over the hole. There will be a tap in the wall nearby and a small bucket for flushing. Fill the bucket with water and pour it down the hole.

In both cases, the doors do not always lock, so exercise caution. Try a polite call of 'Hello?' or knock before bursting in through the door on someone. The etiquette is to leave the door wide open afterwards, to show it's obviously not in use. Also, other than in tourist accommodation, toilet roll is rarely provided. There is seldom any soap either. Bringing your own – hand sanitiser is more convenient than soap – is essential. Package trips may include toilet roll but check if unsure. It's usually possible to buy toilet roll at the Toubkal refuges but it is not cheap.

In the absence of toilets, you'll need to find a rock to squat behind. Here is an example of the rock most people were using at Azib Likemt.

The toilet rock at Azib Likemt

A brief guide to toileting outdoors

Your simple toilet kit should include:

1 Hand sanitiser.
2 Toilet roll – many people use mini packs of tissues as they're sturdier and easier to carry.
3 A small plastic bag to carry out used loo roll. Dog poo bags or coloured sandwich bags work well.

Keep all three in the side pocket of a rucksack or somewhere easily accessible but separate. In lots of areas, you would be advised to bring a small trowel for digging a hole. But the rocky nature of the High Atlas sometimes makes this impractical.

Now to find a good toilet spot. You are looking for:

1 Somewhere out of sight (be sure no one is approaching from another direction).
2 Somewhere away from where most people will walk, e.g. not on or right beside a path and away from your campsite and any other group's campsite.
3 A spot at least 20m away from rivers or other water sources. Human waste contains all sorts of bacteria and even parasites, and this distance means nothing harmful can filter into the river. To go any closer is like defecating in the kitchen sink or, worse, into the pipework that feeds the tap.

Never leave loo roll on the ground. It is one of the biggest misconceptions that toilet paper biodegrades. As for solids, try to find a spot where you can dig a hole. Make it as deep as you can and cover up your waste (not toilet roll!) with the soil you removed. If you're really desperate and can't dig a hole due to the terrain, cover it however you can to stop people stepping in it or animals getting at it. Your other option is to bag it like dog poo and carry it out. If that sounds horrific, then be sure to make proper use of toilets when they're available.

SAFETY AND RISK

Animals

There are no big mammals to watch out for in the High Atlas. Since the 1960s, the barbary lion is no longer found in Morocco. In summer, scorpions and snakes can be found at lower altitudes, including the viper (poisonous) and the Schokari sand racer (harmless). But you are unlikely to see them and they are uninterested unless provoked. Do not put your hands into gaps between rocks, where they like to live, and pay attention to the path so you don't accidentally step on a snake basking in the sun. Although they are not wildlife, it is almost impossible to avoid the many mules passing close by on the trail daily should you have any allergies relating to horses.

There are feral cats and dogs in the villages and it is possible that a dog could have rabies, but it is unlikely. At the time of writing there are at least a couple of mountain dogs who join groups on treks for days at a time, seemingly for the company alone. Apparently, they even summit Toubkal occasionally. Remember these are independent, if surprisingly well-behaved, animals and try not to get too attached.

People

Tourists get a lot of attention when walking through shopping areas – be it in Marrakech or Imlil. You may feel hassled, but you can always keep moving while you politely refuse. If it's really bad in Marrakech, not making eye contact can help. In the quieter mountain villages, you may attract the attention of children more than anyone. See the 'Money' section for advice on how to handle this. However, in general, people are very friendly and hospitable.

It is unlikely that you will experience theft outside of the main tourist areas and even then, it is not particularly common. Guides will often offer a left-luggage service, allowing you to leave any extra belongings that you don't want to carry up the mountain at your accommodation. This may feel unsafe because, generally, there are no lockers and you are simply leaving your bags in someone's house. But I have never heard of any belongings going missing through this arrangement. The whole industry is based on trust and reputation, so theft would not only mean a loss of those qualities but also of income and livelihood.

In the refuges there are no locked doors and most rooms are big dorms with lots of people coming and going. Like all mountain huts, this system works only on a level of mutual trust. That said, it's better to be safe than sorry. Do not leave expensive electronics or money lying about unattended. Keep all of your belongings together in your area so they don't accidentally get packed by someone else in the dark at 3am (odd socks, I'm looking at you). Storing all of your belongings either in a rucksack or in a single dry bag works well. You can tuck the dry bag inside your sleeping bag when you're not using it. You may also like to keep valuables on your person or in a small dry bag that can be easily taken with you to meals, etc. In tents, it's fine to leave belongings in rucksacks out of sight and mind while you are all at camp.

Solo female travel

There is no denying that Western culture is very different to Moroccan culture in its approach to women. Of course, attitudes and norms are changing all the time, but one of the most commonly asked questions about adventure in Morocco is the safety of women. The High Atlas area and Marrakech are much more traditional and conservative than a lot of the rest of the country. If you look womanly and wear fitted clothing you will probably receive unwanted attention (unlike in other parts of Morocco). Similarly, low-cut tops and

Hazy view east from the café on the pass (Toubkal Circuit, Stage 1)

shorts above the knee are inappropriate. Ideally, long trousers and sleeves should be worn, but if you find this too hot, at least cover your shoulders and knees. There is no expectation for female tourists to wear a head scarf. If you do go swimming, try to cover up as much as you can too and don't lie around in a bikini. In a culture where only a husband can see his wife's skin, this behaviour will be deemed as scandalous and will attract a lot of uncomfortable attention. It is also worth knowing that wet hair has insalubrious connotations for Muslims and it's not common to walk around with wet hair in public.

If you are concerned for your safety as a woman, go as part of a large group or make sure you have at least one bloke with you (no matter how mild mannered!). All this said, in my personal experience (having a fairly boyish frame and very long hair) travelling in groups, I have never experienced anything negative myself. The most uncomfortable I have felt was seeing local men pull up chairs to watch and take photos of a group of unaware university students who were lying around in bikinis at Lake Ifni. But, personally, I would not choose to travel alone with just a guide and a cook. Of course, you don't have to take on board these suggestions – you will see many tourists who don't. Equally, you're on holiday and you have the right to relax!

Cultural sensitivities

In terms of clothing, the rules for men are similar to those for women: T-shirts are fine but going shirtless is not appropriate; long shorts are no problem. On occasions, you may also find that local men will address a man in the group first rather than a woman – even if she is in charge.

Photography is another sensitive issue. Do not assume that local people are happy to be photographed, even in the background of a shot. Some nomadic people believe that having their photo taken will steal their soul away. Always ask – or ask your guide for help in asking permission. If they say no, respect that.

ACCIDENTS AND FIRST AID

Given that Toubkal National Park is fairly remote and without much infrastructure, it is worth being prepared for any minor incidents that might occur. How big a first aid kit you carry will depend upon the length of your trip and your objectives. Don't assume that your guide will have one. You can buy compact first aid kits specifically for trekking.

Slips, trips and falls are possible on some of the rougher, less used paths, or simply by bad luck. The ground can often be loose and made up of lots of scree-like stones. Similarly, cuts and scrapes can easily happen. Bring at least a few plasters just in case. Don't forget blister plasters too, if you use them. Although you can buy over-the-counter pain relief in Moroccan pharmacies, you could pack some just in case, such as ibuprofen or paracetamol. You might also like to include antihistamines for hay fever or other minor allergic reactions.

The main hazards that the average hiker needs to be aware of are hot and cold injuries: hypothermia, hyperthermia and dehydration. Hypothermia happens when the body gets too cold, causing it to slowly shut down as the core temperature drops. This is a very long scale. Look out for the 'umbles': grumble, fumble, mumble, stumble, tumble. When your body temperature starts to drop, you become less aware of what is happening around you, so keep an eye on your teammates for signs of unusual behaviour. For example, if they are wearing only a base layer in a blizzard but keep saying they feel warm enough, insist they put on more clothes. Or if they want to curl up and stop/sleep, encourage them to keep moving – movement is the easiest way to get warm.

On the flip side, hyperthermia and heat stroke are caused when the body's core temperature gets too hot. This is far more serious than being too cold. Unlike hypothermia's long, slow descent, overheating gets very serious very quickly. People have been resuscitated from a core temperature of only 13.7°C (normal is 37.5°C), but when the body's temperature rises to just 40°C, the enzymes in your body denature and die. A simple way to prevent this from ever happening is to make sure you drink plenty of water, to allow the body to cool through sweating. Headaches, dizziness, confusion and nausea are all symptoms to watch out for. To cool someone down, sit them in the shade, remove

Treating a lady who collapsed on the slopes of Ikhibi Sud

any excess clothing (e.g. socks) and give them little sips of cold water; too much water in one go and they'll probably vomit. You can also fan them or apply a cold, damp cloth/T-shirt to their skin.

Dehydration can happen in summer or winter. Sometimes it's easier to forget to drink water in winter because you don't feel so obviously thirsty and getting a water bottle out feels like more effort. By not drinking enough water to replace the amount you are losing, you may start to experience headaches and fatigue. In hot weather, dehydration can lead to heat stroke and hyperthermia.

In respect of objective hazards, rockfall is possible though unlikely in the more popular parts of the national park. The few routes where this might be a concern are labelled. In winter, there is no avalanche forecast. You'll have to rely on the local knowledge of your guide, as well as checking the weather forecast in the run-up to your trip and making observations on the day. Avalanches occur when unstable layers in the snowpack, created during the freeze-thaw cycle, break away. They are most likely to occur on 25–45-degree convex slopes. Deep, fresh snowdrifts or a sudden thaw can make avalanches more likely. For more information, there are a lot of good avalanche awareness resources online.

ALTITUDE

Altitude is the height of a point or object, specifically in relation to sea level. As we climb to increasing altitude, there is less oxygen in the air – this is what is meant by the term 'thin air'. But despite there being less oxygen, we still need to deliver the same amount of oxygen to our muscles to keep climbing the mountain. Therefore, reduced oxygen levels directly affect how quickly we can move and are why you see and read about teams of people shuffling to the top of the world's highest peaks. It's not only because they are tired but also because the altitude makes it physically difficult to move.

Your body can start to feel the effects of altitude at heights as low as 2000m but definitely over 3000m. Toubkal is 4167m and the Base Camp refuges sit at 3200m. Most people will notice a faster heart rate, including while at rest. This is not just you being unfit as you slog up a mountain – although it may feel like it! Your body is simply compensating for the lack of oxygen by pumping what it has available around your system faster.

As you climb higher, your body requires more red blood cells to transport oxygen. Once it has made more red blood cells and you are able to pump more oxygen to your muscles, you're acclimatised. Of course, this is only effective as long as you stay at that altitude. Climb even higher and the process starts again.

Path through screes on descent (Toubkal Circuit, Stage 2)

Altitude sickness (sometimes called acute mountain sickness) is what happens when you climb faster than your body can acclimatise. There are many stages to watch out for, but the best solution to altitude sickness is simple: descend to a lower altitude. A good way of tracking your acclimatisation progress is to use a pulse oximeter. These are relatively cheap to buy and measure the oxygen saturation of your blood by clipping onto a finger. If you're above 95% you're doing well.

EMERGENCY RESCUE

A fledgling mountain rescue service, made up of local guides with some advanced training, is in operation in the Toubkal area. There should be a basic stretcher stored at the CAF refuge. However, unlike in many mountainous regions, there is no emergency phone number to call for immediate rescue. You must raise the alarm in person, and nearby guides will try to help. If no one is close by, go to the nearest manned location – for example, to your refuge or back to a café you have just passed. They will help to raise the alarm.

In the event of a rescue, evacuation by helicopter is not available. The casualty would have to be carried down to the closest trail then placed on a mule to be taken down to a valley before travelling to hospital. This is a long and slow process.

In terms of rescue cover, it is important to ensure that your insurance policy covers the relevant activity (hiking, trekking, mountaineering), the location (mountains in Morocco)

CAUTION ADVISED

Several guides have told me the story of a Swiss woman who fell through a cornice on the south side of Tizi n'Toubkal (the south col of Toubkal, approximately 3950m). To save you flipping to the route sections, this side of Toubkal is a series of sheer cliffs and it is challenging to access even in summer. The woman survived the fall, dug a snow hole and spent the night in it before she was found the next day. Some say it was three days, but you get the point. A fairly simple mistake like stepping too close to an edge can suddenly become a life-or-death situation. That's not to say you can't enjoy yourself – but it is important to be aware of the potential risks.

and the altitude (above 4000m). The British section of the Austrian Alpine Club, the AAC(UK), provides rescue insurance as part of its membership, which includes mountainous areas worldwide up to 6000m as standard. It also gives you reciprocal rights, i.e. discounts, at CAF refuges. Note that the AAC(UK) is a catch-all for anyone outside of Austria and includes members worldwide. Other alpine clubs offer similar discounts and can point you towards a good mountain insurance provider if they don't offer their own. Check yours to see how they can help. In any case, make sure you know how to activate your insurance claim in the event of an emergency; often this has to be carried out either before or as help is being called or they won't pay out.

FOOD AND DRINK

There is a far stronger culture of eating than walking in Morocco, and you will be well fed during your time in the mountains. You can easily expect four meals a day: breakfast, lunch, dinner and mid-afternoon tea (with popcorn and biscuits or, if you are lucky, pancakes). On a long trekking day you might also get a small packed lunch on top of that too. Some people choose to go vegetarian as a group to reduce any risk posed by unrefrigerated meat, particularly on multi-day treks.

When you are trekking or camping, food is eaten on the floor. A carpet is laid on the ground, with futon mats around the edges providing a comfortable seating area. Note that it is rude to wear your boots or outdoor shoes on this carpet. Do not be surprised if your guides do not eat with you in the evening: they will wait until after the last call for prayer. There are a few small cafés alongside popular trails – these are mentioned in specific route descriptions. In most cases, these cafés are tiny stick-roofed buildings with plastic tables and chairs outside. They serve mint tea, fresh orange juice or bottled drinks.

What kind of food to expect

For breakfast, you will have a bowl of ready-cut bread with a selection of jams, honey, chocolate spread and peanut butter. There is usually some sort of soft cheese (square or triangle) and there may be yoghurt, boiled eggs and/or porridge. For drinks you can expect instant coffee, cocoa, black tea bags and powdered milk on the table, with hot water provided – and, of course, mint tea.

For lunch, there will be a Moroccan salad, bread, maybe a Berber omelette or lentils or both. Perhaps a plate of pasta, rice or couscous too. A packed lunch may consist of a simple sandwich – either cheese or some sort of tinned fish, maybe with sliced tomato or peppers – and fruit and nuts.

Dinner always starts with a bowl of soup. The main course usually consists of a tagine plus a heaped plate of some sort of carbohydrate, like pasta, rice or couscous. A tagine is a North African dish of spiced vegetables (e.g. potato, carrot, squash) and maybe chicken or beef, cooked in a conical earthenware dish, also called a tagine. There is usually a final course of fruit: oranges, bananas, melons and apples are all common.

Generally, dietary requirements can be catered for if you give your guide enough advance notice. However, it may be very difficult if you have serious allergies, as precise food hygiene is not possible.

In terms of potential health risks, most advice for Morocco suggests avoiding anything that might have

Breakfast at a dar in Imlil (although pretty, this is not a standard breakfast for the trip!)

Couscous and tagine

been washed in unclean water, such as salad or fruit. However, in practice there is no problem with eating the salads or fruit prepared in the mountains. Similarly, it's best to avoid unpasteurised milk, which includes milkshakes and ice creams that aren't pre-packaged.

Water is another area where you need to be careful. Never assume that a tap contains drinking water unless it is explicitly labelled so. To reduce your dependency on bottled water, it's well worth bringing either filters or purification tablets designed for hiking. Make sure to find ones that include protection from Giardia, as this waterborne parasite is prevalent in Morocco. Bilharzia also exists. On the trek, large amounts of bottled drinking water will be included as part of the food provision. While staying at the Toubkal refuges, you can buy bottled water from the shop in Les Mouflons. However, people do purify the tap water – you will need a flexible bottle to do this in Les Mouflons, but there are deep sinks in the CAF refuge. Boiling water kills pathogens, so it is fine to drink tea and other hot drinks. For cold drinks, choose either fruit juice that is squeezed in front of you or something in a sealed bottle.

MONEY

The currency in Morocco is the Moroccan dirham, denoted MAD externally and Dh internally. It is a closed currency and cannot be legally taken out of the country nor bought on foreign exchange. (But don't panic if you have a few coins left in your pocket at the end of the trip; you won't be stopped by the police!) Morocco is

MINT TEA

Tea

Mint tea is an institution in this part of Morocco. It is brewed in a shining silver tea pot, with a long spout, and served in glass cups on a silver tray. These cups are often quite small and look a bit like shot glasses, so you can understand how it might have gained the affectionate name of Berber Whiskey. Sometimes mint tea is prepared with sugar already in the pot, at other times with sugar on the side. If, like me, you don't normally drink tea and don't like mint, the sugar does help to make it bearable. Although you don't always have to accept tea, it does feel quite rude to consistently say no to this symbol of hospitality. Tea is always free. It is important to pour the tea from as high as you can above the cup; as the saying goes, 'No tea without bubbles.'

still very much a cash-based society. You might find places where you can pay by card in Marrakech or in other big cities, but not at all in the mountains – with the exception of local carpet co-operatives. There are foreign exchanges at Marrakech airport and an ATM just before the final exit doors. Marrakech itself has plenty of banks and ATMs, even in the medina. There is an ATM in Asni outside the bank, but the bank is not open every day and the ATM can run out of cash. Typically, you can withdraw a couple of thousand dirham in a single transaction.

Dirhams come in coins and notes. The largest notes are 200dh, followed by 100dh, 50dh and 20dh. Most small shops dislike splitting 200dh or 100dh notes (so you might need to go to a bank to get these changed into coins). It is not a good idea to flash large wads of these high-value notes, especially when paying for things, as it makes you seem like an easy target. Coins come in the values of 10dh, 5dh, 2dh, 1dh, 0.50dh and 0.2dh. These are used for making most purchases.

Local shops in places like Imlil and Asni won't accept euros as payment, although they are quite commonly accepted in Marrakech. However, many local guides, especially the smaller companies, prefer to be paid in euros. It may even be possible to pay in dollars or pounds. This can be done in cash or by an online payment link (obviously, exercise common sense and caution here). This means you can pre-pay the bulk of your trip costs in a more easily available currency then take out a small amount of dirham for other purchases. Note that the mountain refuges play fast and loose with currency. There is a 'mountain exchange rate' of 100dh = 10 euros, and if you pay in one currency, you can expect a mix of currencies in your change. It is always cheaper to pay in dirham.

A selection of dirham coins and notes

Bartering

As much as bartering is a big part of Moroccan culture, there is a time and a place for it. You can't barter for the price of a coffee in the CAF Toubkal, but certainly some of the shops on the streets of Imlil and all of the souks of Marrakech have flexible pricing. This can feel completely alien and even rude to visitors coming from more-reserved Western cultures. The first price you are given will be well above its true value. You can start a counter offer at a third of the suggested price and work up to a compromise. For those uncomfortable with the idea of bartering, think of it as shopping in a corner shop or garage/gas station, where they mark up prices because they can. Bartering gives you the opportunity to reduce it to a more reasonable price. Or you can just pay it.

Camping beside Lake Ifni (Toubkal Circuit, Stage 4)

Tipping

Local children may try asking for money or sweets. This is less common in Imlil, but if you visit much smaller and less touristy villages within Toubkal National Park it is something to be aware of. You may be literally followed through the village by a stream of small children calling 'Bonjour' and asking for bonbons (sweets) or *argent* (money). There is no harm in saying bonjour back to them, but it's best not to give them anything as it encourages begging.

There was no culture of tipping in Morocco, but tourism seems to be slowly creating one. Of course, people are always pleased to receive a tip, but they are well paid for their work and it should not be expected. In restaurants, 10% is exceedingly generous.

CHARGING, PHONES AND PHOTOGRAPHY

The electrical sockets in Morocco take a plug with two round pins. USB ports in wall chargers are not common. If you are spending a few days or longer in the mountains, it is a good idea to bring some sort of power pack, as charging options are limited. This is especially true on the Toubkal Circuit and at the refuges in winter. You can expect to find plugs for charging in most accommodation in Imlil and Aremd, as well as in Amsouzert. There are a small number of charging points at the Toubkal refuges, but the power is not always on. It is still worth printing important travel and bookings documents before you travel, just in case.

Some accommodation in Imlil has Wi-Fi but most doesn't. The CAF

Toubkal has limited Wi-Fi and you can use it if you are staying there or stopping by for a coffee. Not everywhere has phone signal. Decent coverage can be found in Imlil and in the surrounding villages in the valley. But, for example, the Les Mouflons reception phone is an old Nokia taped to a window in the dining room to get signal. Mobile phone coverage is making its way into the more remote valleys – you may spot the red-and-white-striped masts, but do not assume you can access it.

For most visitors, using their own phone contract and data abroad is very expensive. Look into eSIMs or consider getting a Moroccan SIM card for a longer stay. You can buy eSIMs online or a local SIM card at Marrakech airport (past all the checks, on the left-hand side in front of the exit doors). The international prefix for Morocco is +212 and mobile numbers start 06. In the event of an emergency, call 150 for medical help and 190 for the police.

Finally, some notes on photography. To fly a drone anywhere in Morocco, you must get permission from the Directorate General of Civil Aviation. If not, you will be fined and your equipment will be confiscated. There is much confusion about whether it is okay to bring tripods and other camera equipment. As long as you don't arrive with bags full of cameras, lenses and tripods, i.e. looking like a photojournalist, this shouldn't be a problem. If you get extra insurance

Toubkal, left, and Dome d'Ifni from the flank of Ouanoukrim (Route 12)

for your belongings, make sure to read the small print about how to make a claim. Many insurance policies are simply incompatible with being in the mountains, for example, requiring you to file a lost property report with a police log number within 24hr.

MAPS AND NAVIGATION

If you are used to comprehensive, accurate maps of mountains, then you might be in for a shock. The mapping of the High Atlas is very basic. Most maps disagree on fundamentals like the names of peaks and how they are spelt, as well as their heights. Most will show contour lines but no crag markings at all – fairly important in such steep terrain. For the Toubkal region, there are a few options, including Editorial Piolet and Orientazion hiking maps. The Oxford Alpine Club (OAC) maps, used with some alterations for the mapping in this guide, do show the crags. They come in scales of 1:25000 and 1:50000.

Although the Toubkal area is probably covered by your favourite navigation app or online mapping tool, be very careful. They will have basic base maps with the same issues as mentioned for printed maps, but the detail shown can often be wrong. This is especially true for paths. I have seen rock-climbing routes marked with a friendly dotted line – beware! GPS devices can also have difficulty locating due to the steep and deep valleys.

Waymarking in Toubkal National Park is non-existent beyond the occasional row of cairns. Certainly, there are no signposts or direction markers. Faded red and white paint marks, like those used to mark long-distance trails across Western Europe, are only found on the trail between Imlil and Toubkal Base Camp.

GPX tracks for the routes in this guidebook are available to download free at www.cicerone.co.uk/1199/GPX.

LANGUAGE

In Morocco, if a local person speaks English, it is generally their fourth language. Showing willing by learning even a small number of basic words in the native language will be well received. If you do not speak any Amazigh languages nor Arabic, it does help to know French as soon as you step off the tourist highway. French is the business language of Morocco, and many schools teach in French, so brushing up helps. You only need to be sufficient, not proficient.

The Berber people (properly Amazigh, although most in the Toubkal area do refer to themselves as Berbers with tourists) have several different languages. There are three main ones in Morocco: Tachelhit, Tamazight and Tarifit. In this region of the High Atlas, people speak Tachelhit. See Appendix A for a list of common words and their translations.

HUT READING

A HISTORY OF MOUNTAINEERING IN MOROCCO

Of course, this is not, and cannot be, a comprehensive list of the people who have been involved in climbing the mountains of Toubkal National Park and shaping its mountaineering history – not least because records of mountain climbing only go back to the late 1800s. Toubkal was almost certainly climbed before by the local inhabitants of the high valleys.

Still, I have pulled out a few names who I have encountered time and again as I researched this book. Through the archived pages of the *Alpine Journal* and *La Montagne*, I feel like I am walking in their footsteps and in many ways you are too.

Édouard Marie René Bardon, Marquis de Segonzac (1867–1962) – the marquis was a French army officer, explorer and pilot. An entertaining first-person account of some of his undercover travels across Morocco was published in *The Wide World Magazine* in 1902. But, sadly, I cannot find any accounts of his time in the Toubkal region of the High Atlas. However, we do know that in 1923 he became the first foreigner to climb Toubkal, alongside Vincent Berger and Hubert Dolbeau. He was also the first president of the Moroccan section of the Club Alpin Français.

Joseph Dalton Hooker, John Ball and George Maw – these three men mounted a British botanical expedition into the Toubkal area, the first to gain such permission, with some climbing thrown in for good measure. Generally credited with the first scientific exploration of the Toubkal region, they wrote about their climbs in the *Alpine Journal* and wrote a book, *Journal of a Tour in Marocco and the Great Atlas*, which was published in 1878.

Louis Neltner (1903–1985) – this French geologist and mountaineer famously wrote of the High Atlas, 'Il n'est plus beau ni moins beau que les Alpes, il est autre.' (It is not more nor less beautiful than the Alps, it is other.) Reading his accounts in the alpine journals makes you feel like he was one of the driving forces behind the development of mountaineering in Morocco – he is so passionate. He was also a major funder of the first Toubkal refuge, built over the course of a month in the summer of 1939 and later named in his honour.

Jacques de Lépiney (1896–1941) – another key player in exploring and documenting the Toubkal area, this French mountaineer co-wrote a guidebook with Jean Dresch, *Le Massif du Toubkal*, which was published in French by the Moroccan Tourist Office (first edition 1938, second 1942). It was the first book of its kind. The original

CAF refuge built below Tazaghart was named in his honour.

'They [the first mountaineers] had started with many misgivings, little thinking they would find anything of Alpine interest, but they soon had the pleasant surprise of discovering a new range bearing no resemblance to the mountains of Europe. Everything excited their admiration; the glens and gorges cleaving the slopes of the great peaks, covered with an unusual vegetation… the ascents themselves up shattered ridges or gloomy rock walls so different from those of the Alps.' – *The Alpine Journal*, November 1927, Jacques de Lépiney.

Théophile-Jean Delaye (1896–1970) – was a French mountaineer, cartographer and artist. He was stationed in Morocco from the mid-1920s, and was tasked with creating better, more detailed maps of the Toubkal area in the 1930s. Some of his sketches appear in the 1938 guidebook, and his artwork of Moroccan landscapes is striking.

Timeline

1871 – Hooker, Ball and Maw make an expedition to the Toubkal region.
1888 – Joseph Thomson stands on Tizi n'Likemt and hypothesises that the mountain he sees (Toubkal) is the highest in the region.
1912 – Morocco comes under French protectorate rule.
1922 – The CAF Maroc is founded.
1922 – The Marquis de Segonzac climbs another peak, thinking it is the highest. It is later established that Toubkal is indeed the higher peak.
1923, 12 June – The first recorded ascent of Toubkal by foreigners is made by the Marquis de Segonzac, Vincent Berger and Hubert Dolbeau.
1924 – Belay, Maurice de Prandières and colleagues climb Toubkal with a theodolite to measure its precise height.
1929 – Bentley Beetham becomes the first British person to climb Toubkal (or possibly earlier, in 1926, depending on sources).
1931, 8 August – The metal summit pyramid, a trigonometric point, is erected on top of Toubkal.
1937 – The 1:20,000 map of the Toubkal Massif is completed.
1938 – *Le Massif du Toubkal*, the first guidebook to the area, is published.
1938 – The Neltner refuge, the first at what would become Toubkal Base Camp was built over a month during the summer. It had 17 beds, a living room and 1 toilet.
1942 – Toubkal National Park was established.
1956 – Morocco gains independence from France.
1969 – An aircraft crashes on Tibherine.
1973 – The Neltner Refuge is expanded to add an extra dorm room.
1999, 22 November – The new CAF Toubkal refuge opens.
2007 – Les Mouflons refuge opens.

Common plants (clockwise from top left): spurge laurel, Cladanthus scariosus*, thistle, brittle sandwort (*Arenaria pungens*), walnut, spiny madwort (*Alyssum spinosum*)*

BEYOND THIS BOOK

This guidebook focuses on the basics of hiking and trekking in the Toubkal area. But as anyone who has ever looked at a map of the region or stared out into the distance from any of the summits in the book will know, this is only a taste of what is on offer. Especially if you have some expertise in winter. Ski touring, ski mountaineering, ice climbing and winter alpinism are all possible when the conditions are right. The challenge lies in finding local guides who are well enough equipped in both kit and knowledge to take you on your routes. But they do exist and more will come with time. Both the CAF refuge and the Bureau des Guides in Imlil already offer ski guides.

For summer hikes and treks, I have tried to drop hints as to where you might start to extend beyond the remit of this book. There are certainly other valleys that open up access to quieter corners of Toubkal National Park. There are other refuges and Imlil is not the only starting point for adventures – though it is the most convenient for Toubkal. For those who know how, there is plenty rock climbing and roped scrambling in the area, again somewhat hampered by whether you can find a guide to accompany you.

Further afield, Morocco has huge opportunities for adventure and outdoor sports. This book touches on only a small section of the High Atlas mountains, but the Anti-Atlas, Middle Atlas and Rif mountains are all located within Morocco. M'Goun (4071m), the highest peak outside of the Toubkal range, is a popular objective, while Todra Gorge is making a name for itself among rock climbers and has a via ferrata. Jbel Sirwa in the Anti-Atlas, often seen in the far distance from the routes in this book, can be hiked. For anyone in search of a very big adventure, look up Michael Peyron's Grand Traverse of the Atlas route.

Meanwhile on the coast, Essaouira is a growing surf destination, with long sandy beaches and regular waves. Bikepacking and cycle touring are also becoming more common in Morocco. There is a rock-climbing scene starting in Tafraoute, and it is possible to find trail-running trips and itineraries.

All in all, if I've done my job right, you'll have had a fantastic time in Morocco and be back for more. After my first trip to Toubkal, I caught something in Marrakech and was so ill I couldn't look at the trip photos for a month after without feeling sick. But there is just too much to do in Morocco and too many great adventures to be had to let that experience put me off for long. I certainly hope to spend much more time exploring the mountains of Morocco and you can find my extra notes, trip reports and tales at www.travellinglines.com.

If this book has helped you – or if you have suggestions for improvement – please leave a review wherever you buy your books. The more people who know about this book, the more people will arrive in Morocco well informed before climbing Toubkal. It takes 60 seconds to leave a review and, in the case of people who would have otherwise been taken in by the marketing and tried to summit in two days during winter, you may genuinely be saving someone's life. Thank you. Personally, I'd also love to hear how your trip went, either in your review or through the contact details on my website. Or you can tag me in your photos online – whatever works. Have fun and good luck!

'Les hommes ont oublié cette vérité,' dit le renard. 'Mais tu ne dois pas l'oublier. Tu deviens responsable pour toujours de ce que tu as apprivoisé.'
Antoine de Saint-Exupéry, Le Petit Prince

Hiking in the gorge (Toubkal Circuit, Stage 5)

WINTER

Windy conditions inside the gully (Route 4)

INTRODUCTION

If you know how to survive and thrive in winter mountain conditions, Toubkal National Park becomes very appealing in winter. As we've discussed, winter conditions do vary, but with good snow coverage these mountains are transformed: loose rock is replaced by a smooth snow slope. Many people are tempted to climb Toubkal as a very basic introduction to winter mountaineering. This can be a steep learning curve, but it is possible with the right group as long as the altitude is respected.

The following routes cover all the classic one-axe routes from Toubkal Base Camp. This includes the main climb to Toubkal from Imlil, which takes two days – the first day being from Imlil to Base Camp and the second from Base Camp to the summit. There are a couple of options for the ascent route (both the north and south cwm). Then there are suggestions for other routes that may be used for acclimatisation or as alternative objectives when weather conditions don't permit access to the high peaks or ridges. Ouanoukrim, via its normal route along the east ridge, is another popular ascent.

CONSIDERATIONS

The routes in this book are designed for relative beginners and include only the easiest summit routes. All are rated F in Alpine grades. (If you don't know what this means then don't worry. If you do and want winter routes rated PD, AD or above, then you need a different book.) They also assume that you have consistent snow coverage in the mountains above 2000m. In the case of very dry winters, when there is more path than snow showing, it's possible to follow the route directions in the 'Summer' section of the book – even if the terrain will be a little different underfoot.

Please only use these winter route maps and GPX traces as a rough guide. In winter it is up to you (or your guide) to choose the line of least resistance and most safety through the landscape, based on the visible snow conditions and weather. You'll see the GPX traces are very straight lines to reflect this. Beyond the main thoroughfare from Imlil up Toubkal's south cwm, there may not be any bootpack to follow. Similarly, trails of footprints can be easily filled in by fresh snow.

In the case of very bad weather, the police do stop groups from climbing the mountain – even from Imlil to Base Camp. Be prepared for this and consider what else you might like to do with your time, or your guide will make up some alternative low-level routes for you.

KIT

This is not an exhaustive list of everything you could take into the mountains. However, it is pretty comprehensive and will definitely cover the basics required for a winter ascent of Toubkal.

Winter walking boots – winter boots come in levels of stiffness rated B1, B2 and B3, with B3 being rigid boots that do not bend. B0 refers to summer boots (i.e. fully flexible). Do not use summer boots for the winter routes in this book, even if the crampons do somehow strap on – you will get very cold feet.

Crampons – these are specially made metal spikes that attach to the bottom of winter boots, to allow you to grip on icy snow. They are rated C1, C2 and C3 for stiffness to match boot ratings. For example, a B1 boot takes a C1 crampon. If you try to put a C3 crampon on a B1 boot, the boot will bend but the crampon won't and will fall off instead. You need proper crampons for Toubkal, not microspikes or micro crampons or anything held together by rubber and chains. If at all possible, practise putting on your crampons (and fit them to the size of your boots) before leaving. Do this on a lawn not on your living room carpet…

Ice axe – a single walking ice axe with a straight or slightly curved shaft will be suitable. These are sold in different lengths, depending on your height. The rough rule of thumb is that the spike should graze the top of your winter boot when held loosely at your side.

Socks – bring at least one pair of thick, warm walking socks and as many spares as you'd like.

Winter kit

Winter hiking trousers – many are fleece lined and slightly water resistant. Warm leggings underneath summer walking trousers can work just as well. Make sure they are quick drying and comfortable.

Warm base layer – look for a long-sleeved, breathable base layer designed for cold weather.

Warm layers (lots) – bring as many fleeces as you think you might need. You might also pack a softshell or insulated jacket.

Spare warm layer – pack an extra fleece or insulated jacket that you are not intending to wear, except at camp or on top of Toubkal!

Underwear – You don't need anything specialist, just make sure they are comfy.

High-factor sun cream – bizarrely, you are even more likely to get burnt in winter. Clear skies, altitude and reflection off the snow all conspire against you. Although you may not have much skin showing, with all your warm layers, do bring a little suncream.

Sunglasses – you will require category 4 mountain sunglasses to protect your eyes from high levels of UV. If you don't have the correct level of protection, you can end up snowblind from the sheer brightness.

Snow goggles – in the event of a blizzard, snow goggles are a good idea for keeping the snow out of your eyes. You might get away with sunglasses but they will offer much less protection.

Gaiters (optional) – gaiters can be worn to keep deep snow out of your boots (the snow gets in, melts and then makes your socks wet). Some winter mountaineering trousers have built-in gaiters to prevent this.

Sterilisation tablets or a filter – water is very hard to come by naturally from Base Camp onwards. You could, in principle, melt snow for drinking water, but this is a lot of hassle and requires bringing a stove. Instead, most groups buy bottled water from their refuge or arrange for it to be brought up. The bottles in the refuge shops are made of thin plastic and freeze very easily.

Water container – you will require at least 1 litre in capacity. Camelbaks are generally not a good idea as the tubes and valves freeze in the very cold conditions. Bring a bottle or, even better, an insulated bottle or flask. That way your water will still be drinkable in the mountains.

Snacks – see the 'Food and drink' section for more details but some snacks from home would be a good idea if you are used to grazing. Some sweets for a little boost halfway up a long ascent can be helpful. Make sure your snacks won't freeze solid.

Waterproofs – even though you will not be expecting rain, waterproof jackets and trousers are very good at repelling snow and wind.

Gloves – as gloves get wet easily, bring at least a couple of pairs – even if they claim to be waterproof. It is hard to dry your kit effectively in either refuge. Mittens are fine as long as you can still hold an ice axe.

Warm hat and/or buff – you lose a lot of heat through your head. A buff or scarf can protect your face from cold wind and horizontal snow.

Sleeping bags or quilts – the refuges are cold in winter and the bedrooms are unheated. Piles of blankets will be available, so at least bring a sleeping bag liner. A winter-rated sleeping bag would make sure you have a warm night's sleep. You can sometimes rent these from providers.

Clothes to sleep in – again, the warmer the better.

Hut shoes (optional) – Les Mouflons will let you wear boots in the corridors; CAF Toubkal will not. Bringing a pair of shoes is not necessary, but you will be more comfortable. It also means you won't have to wear winter boots around Marrakech.

Head torch – as well as a requirement for pre-dawn starts, a head torch is handy when the electricity in the refuge turns off.

Powerpack – there are power sockets in the refuges but in winter the power is barely on.

Hand sanitiser or wipes – these are handy for before meals while trekking and when using the toilets, etc. See the 'Health and hygiene' section for more details.

First aid kit – a small personal first aid kit, or group one, is useful for treating minor ailments/injuries (see the 'Accidents and first aid' section of the guidebook).

Entertainment – if you're spending more than a couple of days at Base Camp, you'll probably have long afternoons in the refuge, especially if the weather is unsettled. Bring a pack of cards, a small packable game or a book.

Powdery snow inside the bowl below Afella and Akioud (Route 4)

ROUTE 1

Imlil to Base Camp

Start	Toubkal trailhead
Finish	Base Camp
Duration	5hr+
Distance	8km (5 miles)
Ascent	1300m (4270ft)
Descent	0m

The first step to climbing Toubkal is the hike from Imlil to Toubkal Base Camp, where the two refuges are sited at 3200m. You will set out from your overnight accommodation in and around Imlil or Aremd. Or if you didn't spend a night there, you may be driven to the trailhead or you may hike up from the centre of Imlil. (Use the summer routes from Imlil to find your way if need be.) Since there are many ways to do this, we'll start from the actual trailhead. The hike from there is almost entirely uphill: although not all steep, it is persistent. You will pass the holy shrine of Sidi Chamharouch and a couple of cafés higher up, which all make good places to stop – if they're open.

There is no particular marking or sign for the trailhead. Start from the highest road bridge over the river across from Aremd. Looking south, you'll clearly see a wide-open rocky plain and beyond, where the valley narrows into the distance. This is the direction you are going. Cross to the west side of the bridge and turn left up the road. In particularly snowy winters, the police checkpoint is the building on the corner.

Once everything has been approved, continue past the checkpoint to reach a gap between two drystone walls on your left, with a footpath between them. Take this footpath and cross the alluvial plain, a flat, barren landscape created by the river. It is very stony underfoot. The trail bears left across the wide-open area then zigzags up the left-hand side of the valley towards a big stone building with a balcony. This is a **police checkpoint**.

Beyond this, the path contours the left-hand side of the Mizane Valley, slowly rising. The summer path is quite wide, so you should have a flat ledge of snow to walk on. However, in deeper snow, the slope is steep with quite a long run-off into the river below. Follow the line of the trail or bootpack, slowly ascending.

Map continues on page 63

The path across the alluvial plain

Soon, you will reach **Sidi Chamharouch**, which may look like a ghost town of empty stalls under a layer of white. The industry that has sprung up around the shrine's visitors and summer trekkers is much quieter in winter, but it will probably not be completely empty, even in the deep winter snow. You should be able to stop here at a café for hot tea (the first you come to on the right of the path has a squat toilet).

SIDI CHAMHAROUCH SHRINE

The tomb of Sidi Chamharouch is said to lie beneath the large, white-painted boulder beside the trail to Toubkal Base Camp. Sidi Chamharouch is the King of the Djinn or Lord of Demons, and it is said he will grant wishes if you bring him gifts and offerings. The waters that flow from the hillside are said to cure ailments. This is a popular pilgrimage site and no tourists are allowed to visit. The site was worshipped pre-Islam and a mosque was built next to the boulder when Islam came to Morocco.

Cross the **bridge** over the river and continue your ascent. The valley turns a corner at Sidi Chamharouch and the route bears roughly south-west. Continue up a short but steep snow slope to gain height on the right-hand side of the valley. Looking back, you might be able to make out the white-painted boulder, which marks the location of the shrine, against the snow.

Unless you are the first hikers after fresh snowfall, there should be a clear bootpack trail in the snow, made by the footsteps of those before you. This moves

The bootpack towards Base Camp

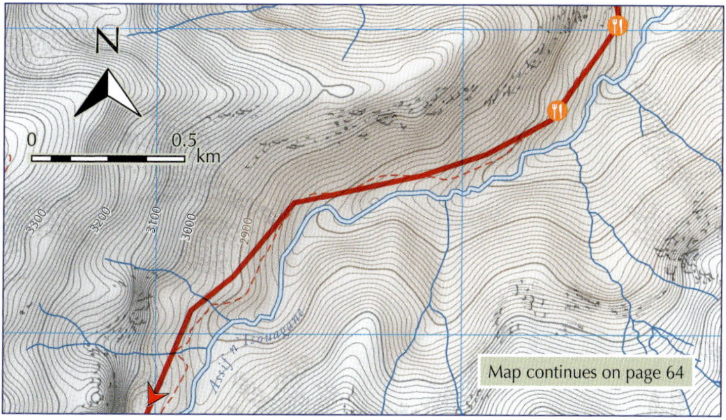

up and down the hillside depending on conditions, but it is generally on the top half of the slope, below the cliffs. As you climb, you'll pass two more **cafés**. These are particularly welcome to duck into out of a blizzard, if they're open.

Finally, make the long traverse, still on the right-hand slope of the valley, to the refuges. You should feel the terrain flattening out eventually as the valley widens – even if you can't see it. Above and to the left are the peaks of Tichki (3737m) and then Afekhoi (3751m). On the right is the long north-east ridge of Aguelzim South (3663m) and beyond it, Biguinoussene (4007m). When the **refuge**s appear out to your left, like a dark castle against the white, don't cut straight across towards them.

Wait until you are almost level with them before turning to avoid the walls and terraces that are clearly visible in summer but probably hiding under snow.

TOUBKAL BASE CAMP

Two refuges now stand in the valley west of Toubkal. The lower refuge is Les Mouflons. The upper, with its distinctive tower, is CAF Toubkal. The open-fronted building to the right as you approach is the remains of the Neltner refuge, which was in use between 1938 and 1999. Beyond this is the police checkpoint. (It may be shut in winter.) If you stand outside either of these refuges and face north, you'll be looking back at the same mountains that stand above Imlil and Tacheddirt, although Imlil itself is out of sight. This view is particularly beautiful with a pale pink sky of sunrise or sunset against the snow. To the west are the formidable flanks of Biguinoussene. As you look south and up the valley, you'll see Tizi n'Ouagane, although you can't see the top. And to the east lies Toubkal. You cannot see the summit, but Ikhibi Sud is the hanging valley directly behind the refuges.

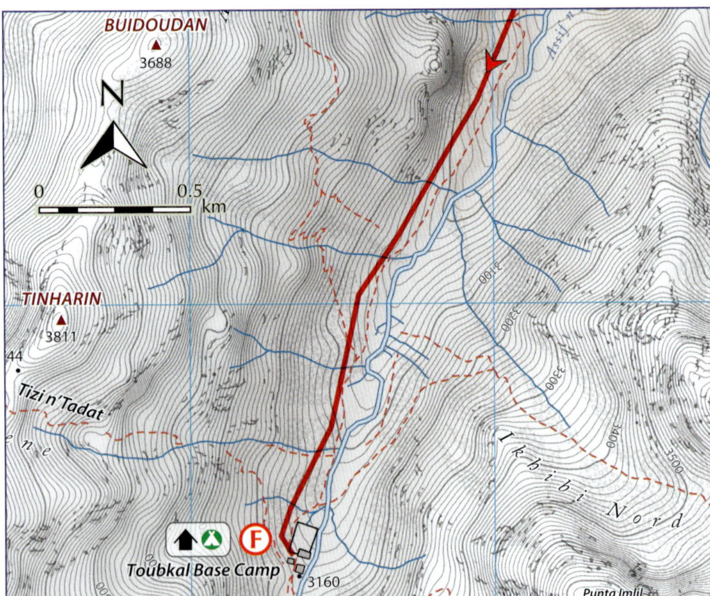

ROUTE 2

Base Camp to Toubkal summit (normal – Ikhibi Sud)

Start/Finish	Base Camp
Duration	6hr; to Toubkal summit 4hr
Distance	3km (2 miles)
Ascent	1000m (3280ft)
Descent	1000m (3280ft) (returning via ascent route)

The ascent of Toubkal via the most common (normal) route is through the south cwm, Ikhibi Sud. The route can be split into three distinct parts: the initial ascent from Base Camp to the cwm, the crossing of the cwm to reach the ridge at Tizi n'Toubkal and the climb along the ridge to reach Toubkal's summit. Many groups set off in the dark to reach the top for sunrise. However, the ascent itself will likely be less busy and more enjoyable in the morning light.

From Les Mouflons, walk south and uphill, passing the CAF Toubkal on your left and the police checkpoint on your right. Continue up the slope beyond the buildings for approximately 100m until the mountain to your left presents an easy-angled slope before the crags. This is the foot of Toubkal. Turn left, heading east, and start to ascend the bottom of this slope, keeping all crags well to your right. As the slope steepens, follow the path of least resistance by traversing in long, shallow zigzags across the convex slope rather than powering straight up. Usually, there will be a bootpack trail marked in the snow from previous groups. Looking back across the valley, you'll get a better view of the ridge opposite: Afella on the left, Biguinoussene on the right and the distinctive Clochetons in between.

As the steepness lessens, you will step out onto the lip of a large cwm. This is **Ikhibi Sud**, the southern cwm of Toubkal. At the lip is a cluster of large boulders, taller than a person, which makes a good spot for a quick break – layers, snacks and water. They also provide a small amount of shelter from the wind. Standing at the rocks looking south-east, you will see the cliffs of Toubkal West rise on your right and the narrow ridge that separates the north cwm from the south cwm on your left. And before you is the shallow bowl of the south cwm itself, with a rising slope into the distance.

TINHARIN
3811
3744
Tizi n'Tadat
Toubkal Base Camp
3160
edge of cwm
Ikhibi Nord
Ikhibi Sud
Punta Imlil
TIBHERINE
3887
Tizi n'Ouanas
IMOUZZER
4010
North Col
TOUBKAL
4167
Aiguille d'Ifni
SE Ridge
Col d'Ifni
3756
Tizi n'Toubkal
Jebel Toubkal
TOUBKAL W.
4030
Tete D'Ouanoums
3970
Ouanoums Ridge
3658
Tizi n'Imouzzer
0
0.5
km

While everyone focuses on Toubkal, its next-door peak, **Toubkal West** (4030m), is a pleasant mountain in its own right. It can be climbed either direct from near the top of Ikhibi Sud (up the slope from the 3850m contour) or via its north-east ridge, which connects to Tizi n'Toubkal. You can add it to your Toubkal ascent or climb it on a separate outing. The north-east ridge is graded F-.

You are aiming for the col (saddle) on the right-hand side of this cwm, where the shoulder of Toubkal West meets the ridge of Toubkal. To reach it, start your ascent up the middle of the cwm, choosing the easiest line. Then, as the slope steepens, veer right towards the upper ridgeline. The very top of this slope is often wind scoured, and the frozen screes of the summer path may be visible underneath. Follow these zigzags or make your own up to the col of **Tizi n'Toubkal**.

Be careful as you arrive – it is a narrow col and can produce a cornice on the outer edge. There is a long, sheer drop on the other side. But from here, weather willing, you should have your first views south and east out of the Base Camp valley, towards Lake Ifni in the near distance and Dome d'Ifni (3876m). The triangular peak with sheer crags facing you, almost directly due east, is Toubkal. You may even be able to see the black quadrupedal pyramid that marks the summit.

Now, turn left, heading east, and follow the ridgeline towards Toubkal. The way is fairly broad at first. Stick to the centre or left-hand side of the ridge, wary of any cornice build up to your right. Again, this initial section can be wind scoured, leaving the summer path visible under a layer of rime ice. Soon the ridge narrows to a rocky arête. The easiest route passes to the left, just below the crest of the ridge on

Looking down Ikhibi Sud

a narrow ledge with a long, steep runout to the left. (Ice axes are recommended!) Beyond this short section, you can regain the top of the ridge as it flattens into the summit plateau. The final climb is a steady, shallow ascent across this plateau, turning a sharp corner right to reach the top. In good visibility, the summit pyramid should peek up into view and spur you on the last hundred metres.

The summit of Toubkal is marked by a distinctive **black metal square-based pyramid** that is several metres high. It was built in 1931 as a triangulation point.

The **summit marker** is close to the southernmost edge of Toubkal, with a sheer drop. Views look out south in a wide east-to-west panorama, covering all the eastern peaks of Toubkal National Park and beyond to the Anti-Atlas and Jbel Sirwa. Dome d'Ifni is directly below, and you can even see as far as the Sahara on a clear day.

Descent options

Most people descend by retracing their steps down Ikhibi Sud to Toubkal Base Camp (**2hr**). It is possible to take in the summit of Toubkal West on this descent if you have the time (add **30–45min** to descent time).

Alternatively, you could descend via the north cwm, Ikhibi Nord (**2½hr**). A cornice on the north edge of Toubkal's summit plateau doesn't always make this a practical descent route. For directions, follow the Ikhibi Nord ascent route in reverse.

The iconic metal pyramid at Toubkal's summit

ROUTE 3

Base Camp to Toubkal summit (alternative – Ikhibi Nord)

Start/Finish	Base Camp
Duration	7hr; to Toubkal summit 4–5hr
Distance	4km (2½ miles)
Ascent	1100m (3610ft)
Descent	1100m (3610ft) (returning via ascent route)

An alternative way to climb Toubkal is via the north cwm, Ikhibi Nord. This is a steeper and longer route, but it allows you to avoid the crowds of people climbing and descending on Ikhibi Sud. You must walk slightly downhill from Base Camp to access the cwm. After that, the climb is a fairly constant ascent until about 3850m, just below Tibherine. The route crosses a shallow section across the North Col before turning right and completing the short scrambly section onto Toubkal's summit plateau. Due to the easy scrambling, steepness and length, it is slightly more difficult than the normal route.

From the refuges, walk downhill along the Imlil tracks, just as far as is necessary to cross the **main river** that runs behind the refuges. Now on the east bank, continue north. You'll see the nose of a ridge coming down from above you, right to left towards the river. Behind this is the entrance to Ikhibi Nord. Stay low, following the river until you've rounded the bottom of this ridge, then turn sharply right and head up the slope towards the jaws of **Ikhibi Nord**.

Stay at the base of the cwm, with steep, jagged cliffs rising on either side. To the left is the craggy flank of Tibherine and on the right is Punta Imlil, rising into the west ridge of Toubkal. The way steepens as you approach the headwall at the back of the cwm, a short cliff face that marks a change in slope aspect. As you look back, the Tadat pinnacle is clear on the horizon – maybe lit by sunrise.

Tibherine is most distinctive for its summit marker: the engine of an aircraft that crashed in 1969. Be wary of cornices when approaching as the engine is wedged right on the edge of the peak. If you see the glint of metal as you climb, this is part of the crash debris that was strewn down Ikhibi Nord. It is usually buried deep under the snow but is visible in summer.

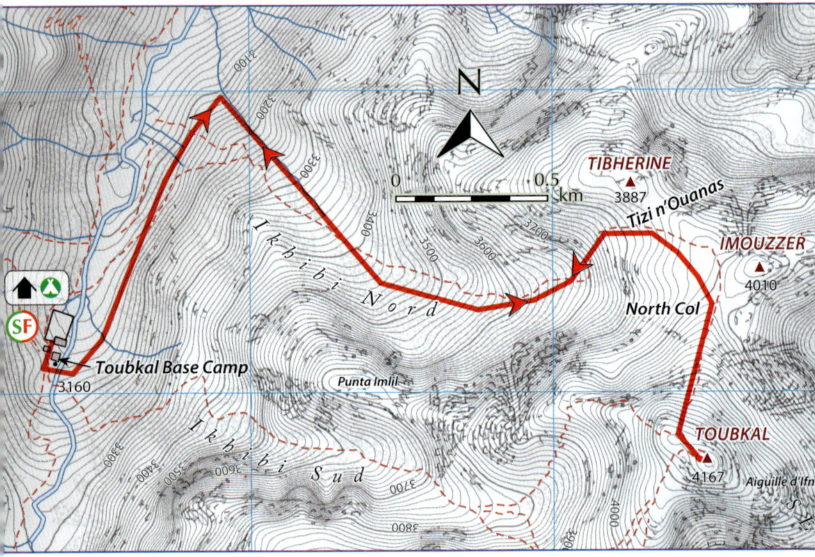

As you reach the foot of the headwall, bear left to pass the cliff on its left-hand side then turn right to correct your course back into the middle of the cwm – not that there's much left of it. The way is much flatter now, becoming a wide bowl between peaks. Imouzzer is the peak directly ahead and Tibherine is on the slope up to the left as you round the headwall.

IMOUZZER

Imouzzer (4010m) technically has three peaks but it is classed as having only two separate summits. You can easily reach the first summit in winter with only a 100m diversion, where there is a particularly good view of Dome d'Ifni (3876m), which is often hidden behind Toubkal. The second summit is separated from the first by a gully approximately 5m deep. This is crossable when filled with snow but otherwise poses a challenge – either an abseil or a difficult downclimb. Depending on the snow conditions, you may be able to return from Imouzzer I the way you came and traverse around to the bottom of the gully from the west. Imouzzer II is reached, beyond the gully, along an exposed ridge. This route is rated F+ in winter and is a rock climb in summer.

Continue up the middle to the **North Col** to the right of Imouzzer. The snow slope that heads steeply up and to the right leads to Toubkal, though you may not be able to see the triangular summit marker from here. Depending on the snow depth, this last section involves scrambling in places (less snow means more hands on rock) and kicks up steeply at the end before topping out on **Toubkal's summit plateau**.

Walk the last few metres to victoriously reach the black pyramidal summit marker. The view south looks out over Toubkal's steep southern cliffs to Dome d'Ifni, directly below. The wide east-to-west panorama covers all of the eastern peaks of Toubkal National Park and beyond to the Anti-Atlas and Jbel Sirwa. You can even see as far as the Sahara on a clear day.

Descend via the way you came (**2½hr**) or, more usually, down the shorter Ikhibi South route (**2hr**) back to the refuges.

Heading north down the valley to Ikhibi Nord

ROUTE 4

Aougdal Bou Tioana gully (acclimatisation hike 1)

Start/Finish	Base Camp
Duration	3hr
Distance	3.5km (2¼ miles)
Ascent	500m (1640ft)
Descent	500m (1640ft)

This short walk can be used as an acclimatisation day or as an alternative to climbing peaks. It involves climbing up a snow gully – the gorge of the river in summer – below the cliffs of Afella (4030m). The gully is wide and shallow, though steep sided, and is a walk not a climb (people ski down it). As you ascend into the cwm below Tizi n'Afella, you will gain views across to Toubkal.

Approaching the gully below the band of cliffs

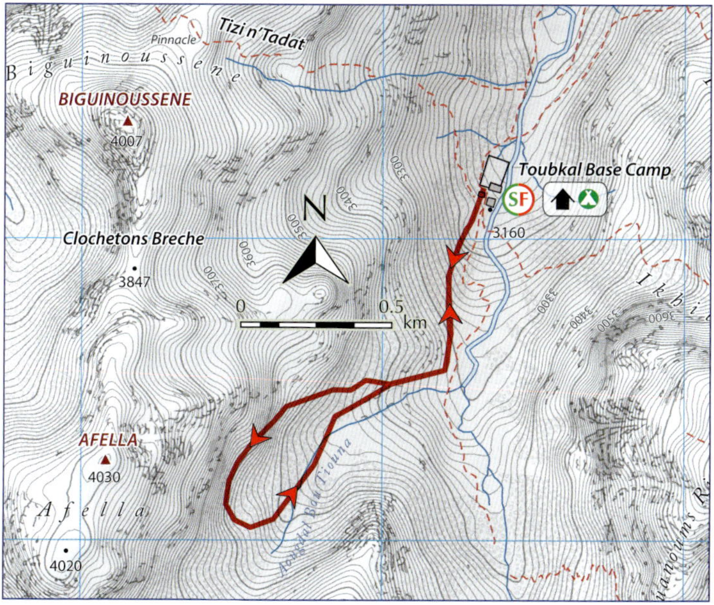

From the Toubkal refuges, head due south and uphill in the middle of the valley bowl. In case of low snow cover, stay towards the right-hand side of the valley, skirting below the cliffs that mark the end of Afella's north-east ridge. This is a fairly shallow ascent, at least compared to climbing any of the peaks.

Before very long, where the slope flattens off, you will come to a band of cliffs on the right-hand side. This low, wide crag has a distinctly different colour of rock to the others nearby – it may seem yellowish or perhaps orange. Just before this crag is a wide, clean-edged gully. Simply turn right up the snow slope and into the bottom of the gully. Be wary in high winds; the gully can funnel the wind if it's blowing in the right direction.

Continue up through the gully, taking the easiest line for the snow conditions, until you exit out into the bowl of the cwm. Above and to the right are the stepped cliffs of Afella's east flank. To the left is the end of the north-east ridge of Akioud (4010m). Staying on the right-hand side of the slope, below the cliffs, climb steadily upwards towards the pass. You won't be climbing all the way to the pass, just making a circuit around the edge of the cwm.

AFELLA

Afella (4030m) is one of the few peaks in Toubkal National Park over 4000m. It has two summits, Afella North and Afella South, and it is quite challenging to summit in winter from the Toubkal side. The easiest access is via Tizi Melloul, which involves a long walk around the mountain (from east to south to north-west). And then, unfortunately, all the way back again to return to Toubkal Base Camp. This is a huge day in winter. The slopes around the south-west side have dizzying run-offs, so present high consequences if you were to slip.

As you reach the back of the cwm, where the ground steepens towards Tizi n'Afella and Akioud, simply veer left and follow the contour around the top of the bowl. This is the high point of the day and you should have good views out west across to Toubkal and Ikhibi Sud. Continue to traverse around to the opposite side of the cwm, below the ridge.

From here, simply descend this side on easy-angled snow slopes to return to the top of the gully. Retrace your steps down the gully and back to the refuges.

Refinding the gully to descend

ROUTE 5

Tizi n'Ouanoums (acclimatisation hike 2)

Start/Finish	Base Camp
Duration	3hr
Distance	2km (1¼ miles)
Ascent	500m (1640ft)
Descent	500m (1640ft) (returning via ascent route)

Despite not being a mountain peak, Tizi n'Ouanoums is an impressive objective in winter. You can climb it from the easy side – accessed in a relatively short walk from the Toubkal refuges. Beyond it is a deeply impressive view. On one side lie the jagged cliffs of Toubkal's south face, black rocks highlighted and outlined by perfectly white snow. In front, the steep view down into the valley draws the eye out to Lake Ifni, a pool of blue catching the sun. And beyond it a long horizon stretches towards Jbel Sirwa and the Anti-Atlas.

From the Toubkal refuges, head due south up the valley as if you were heading for Tizi n'Ouagane. Initially, stay roughly in the middle or to the right as you climb the snow slope, using the north-eastern cliffs of Afella as a distant handrail. As the terrain flattens off, you will see a wide, low band of orange-coloured cliffs on your right. Continue on past these, heading roughly south-east as the main valley rounds a slight corner. The ridgeline dropping down into the valley on your right is the north-east ridge of Akioud.

As the main valley turns back due south to reach Tizi n'Ouagane and the pass between Bou Ouzzal and Ouanoukrim, cut off left towards Tizi n'Ouanoums. This is a distinct notch in the ridge on the horizon, due east. Choose the best route ahead based on the snow cover. Hopefully, there will be an easy-angled snow slope in front of you, all the way up. In this case, aim slightly left of the pass then traverse across to reach it. Alternatively, you could continue a little further up towards Tizi n'Ouagane until you are more level with the height of the pass then traverse gently across to it, approaching from the right. This is mixed ground with some rocks breaking out through the snow – good practice for beginners wanting to test their crampon work, but not an easy line in low snow.

Whichever side you come from, the sharp sides of the pass keep the view a secret until the last moment. As you round the corner, you are suddenly presented

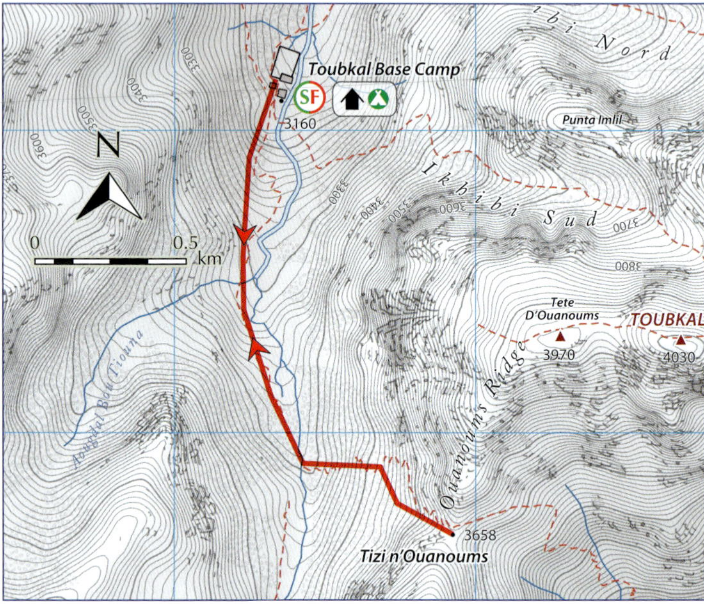

Approaching Tizi n'Ouanoums

The jagged south side of Toubkal and Toubkal West

with an overwhelming panorama of rock and snow: from the back of Toubkal West, across to Dome d'Ifni and the long Adrar Bou Ouzzal ridge and the steep drop into the gorge below. The only colour comes from the blueness of the rime ice and the sparkling pool of Lake Ifni in the distance, catching the light.

Lake Ifni, sometimes Lac d'Ifni, is the only lake in Toubkal National Park. At about 2500m above sea level, it is the highest lake in Morocco and has no visible inflow of rivers. It can be reached in summer by descending the gorge ahead of you (the path zigzags left) and is part of the Toubkal Circuit. In winter, it's hard to believe that mules come up and down this pass in summer.

Behind you, there is also a clear view of Ouanoukrim on the southern (left) end of the ridge opposite. The summer path that descends to Lake Ifni is probably blocked with snow but provides a pleasant ledge to sit on and enjoy the view.

To descend, retrace your steps to return to your refuge.

Descending from Tizi n'Ouanoums back into the Ouanoums valley

ROUTE 6

Ouanoukrim

Start/Finish	Base Camp
Duration	6hr+
Distance	8km (5 miles)
Ascent	1000m (3280ft)
Descent	1000m (3280ft)
Warning	Do not attempt the ridge scramble in high winds. In low visibility, it can be difficult to find the start of the scramble on descent.

Ouanoukrim is the second-highest mountain in the High Atlas, after Toubkal. It has two peaks: Ras (4083m) and Timesguida (4089m). It is situated south west of Toubkal, at the end of the line of mountains on the opposite side of the valley. To reach the two summits involves a short section of scrambling along the east ridge, but most of the ascent is done in reaching the pass below it, Tizi n'Ouagane. The summits themselves are on easy-angled terrain, with Ras being the steeper. This route takes in both peaks, Ras first then Timesguida, but it can just as easily be done in reverse.

From Toubkal Base Camp, walk south, slowly ascending the valley. Stick to the middle or right-hand side, passing the cliffs of Afella and the band of yellowish-orange crag on your right-hand side. Beyond this, traverse to the left and climb up to the pass in the centre of the valley, if snow conditions allow. The last section up to the pass is relatively steep. Beware of overshooting as cornices can build up on the south side.

Pause at the pass, **Tizi n'Ouagane**, to enjoy the view beyond it towards the Anti-Atlas and back the way you've come. The mountain to the east of the pass is Bou Ouzzal. To get onto Ouanoukrim's massif from Tizi n'Ouagane there is a short section of straightforward but unavoidable scrambling. You cannot walk around the scramble. It is only about 100m in length but has sheer drops on either side and should not be attempted in high winds. Note that this is the gateway to the mountain; you must do in reverse whatever you do to ascend.

The isolated peak directly opposite Tizi n'Ouagane is **Bou Ouzzal**. Sadly, this mountain is often forgotten, since it is only 3860m. That said, it is not very far

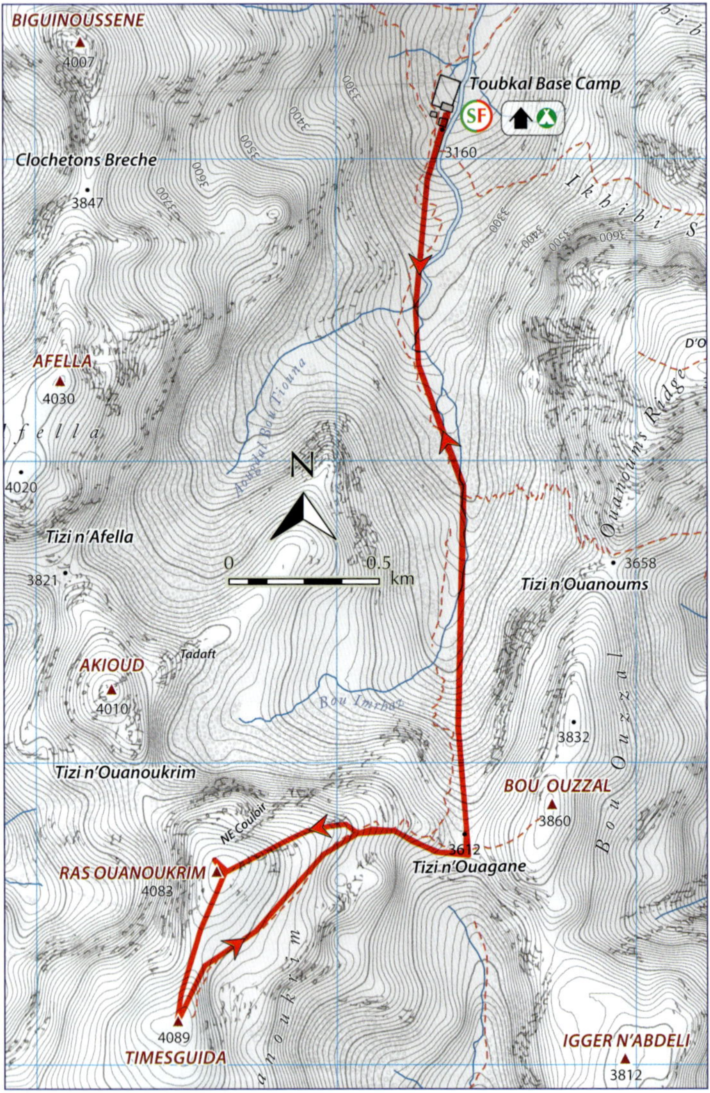

BIGUINOUSSENE
4007
Toubkal Base Camp
SF
3160
Clochetons Breche
3847
Ikhbibi S
AFELLA
4030
Afella
4020
Assif Bou Tiouna
Ouanoums Ridge
D'O
N
0
0.5
km
Tizi n'Afella
3821
3658
Tizi n'Ouanoums
AKIOUD
Tadaft
4010
Bou Imrhar
3832
Tizi n'Ouanoukrim
BOU OUZZAL
Bou Ouzzal
NE Couloir
3860
3612
RAS OUANOUKRIM
Tizi n'Ouagane
4083
Ouanoukrim
4089
TIMESGUIDA
IGGER N'ABDELI
3812

from the pass if you have the time and inclination to take it in. The first two summits are graded F+ in winter, but the traverse beyond that is much harder. Its first recorded ascent was by Bentley Beetham in 1929.

From the pass, head west up the initial slope presented to you. Ahead you should see two pinnacles of rock sticking upright out of the snow like fingers. Pass these on the right then move back towards the left, crossing behind them to regain the ridge. Depending on the snow conditions, this may have more or less visible rock, but scramble upwards, keeping to the middle of the ridge. The scrambling should be easy if slightly exposed, and ice axes are definitely required. After a short distance, the scramble becomes a snow slope. Keep climbing, following the right-hand edge of the mountain as it veers off – but at a safe distance – until the ground flattens.

Continue to follow this line up to what appears to be the summit. The true summit is just beyond and involves a short down-and-up scramble across an arête to reach the true summit of Ras. The arête sits at the top of Ouanoukrim's central couloir (a steep gully) and feels airy as you cross, even if it's only a few steps. The small top of **Ras Ouanoukrim** sits high above Toubkal Base Camp valley, feeling isolated, with steepness on all sides. There are good views of Toubkal West and the craggy south face of Toubkal.

The flank of Ouanoukrim from just below Tizi n'Ouagane

When you're ready, cross back over the arête onto the lower summit. Looking due south, you should be able to see the flat, broad summit of Timesguida. Descend the easy-angled slope off Ras towards it then head up the other side. The highest point is not so obvious as the top is a wide plateau, but there is a small summit marker. You can see clearly across to the back of Akioud, Afella's south summit and, on the far left, the flat top of Tazaghart.

The **Tazaghart Plateau** (3980m) is about 3km^2 and is popular with ski tourers. Its high point is Talat n'Ifri, on the right-hand end of the summit from this viewpoint. Its north face has many ridges and gullies.

To return, cut across the eastern flank of the mountain, slowly descending as you traverse the snow slope back to the top of the scramble. As a very rough guide, aim for Toubkal in the distance. If in doubt, do not drop too low as there are steep and difficult cliffs. Downclimb the scramble, this time passing to the left of the pinnacles, to reach **Tizi n'Ouagane**, then retrace your steps to the refuge.

The Ouanoums valley, looking north

SUMMER

Descending the north ridge of Toubkal (Route 11)

INTRODUCTION

In summer, Toubkal is a non-technical peak surrounded by other interesting mountains. There are plenty of scree slopes but anyone who describes Toubkal National Park as barren doesn't have their eyes open. Or perhaps, in fairness, they are walking in the dark. Although there isn't much grass, all but the high peaks are populated with plants and flowers. There are flocks of mountain goats and Alpine choughs, although the real wildlife tends to hide away from busier areas.

This section of the routes refers to summer in terms of conditions rather than a particular time of year: when you will not expect to encounter snow on the ground – or if so, only in small, isolated patches that can be easily walked around.

The routes in this section start with a choose-your-own adventure for acclimatisation hikes in and around Imlil, taking in at least one waterfall. This is followed by the main climb of Toubkal from Imlil, done over two days. The first step is from Imlil to Base Camp and the next from Base Camp to the summit, with a couple of options for this ascent route (both the north and south cwm). Then, there are further suggestions for other summits, including Ouanoukrim, Aguelzim and all of Toubkal's subsidiary peaks. All of the 4000ers in the area are covered for completeness, although not all are recommended for hikers. Finally, the six-day Toubkal Circuit trekking route is covered in full, with a stage per day.

CONSIDERATIONS

If you get stuck with any of the mountaineering terms, remember there's a full glossary in Appendix A.

It is unusual for groups to abort a hike of Toubkal in the summer. In the case of strong winds, be very wary, especially if you are intending to scramble. There is no shame in changing plans in light of the weather to prevent a high-risk situation.

You may notice that some of the routes are listed as being longer in summer than in winter. This is not a mistake. While in winter you can walk across a slope, following the many zigzags of a summer path is physically longer.

KIT

This is not an exhaustive list of everything you could take into the mountains. However, it is pretty comprehensive and will definitely cover the basics for a summer ascent of Toubkal or a trekking circuit.

Summer walking boots – any ordinary summer walking boots with good grip should be fine. High ankles are advised (boots not shoes) as rescue would be difficult if you rolled an ankle. A waterproof lining isn't necessary but avoid anything with a mesh upper as this will fill with dirt. You might like a bit of an edge to the soles of your boots for scrambling and scree slopes. For this reason, barefoot hiking boots are not advised.

Socks – one pair of walking socks and as many spares as you'd like.

Long summer hiking trousers – lightweight breathable trousers. You might be able to wear knee-length shorts, but zip-offs would be better if you're going to want shorts. This is worth considering if you plan to complete the Toubkal Circuit, as this route passes through rural communities where it is disrespectful to show much skin. Ideally, long trousers should be worn by both men and women.

Base layer – a lightweight, breathable base layer. Long sleeves will help with sun protection but see the 'Cultural sensitivities' section for guidance. Some base layers are sold specifically with SPF ratings (look for 'sun shirts' or 'sun hoodies').

Fleece – a thin fleece to walk in during cooler mornings or evenings and on higher summits. Any jumper is okay. Bring a couple if you know you get cold.

Spare warm layer – a thick fleece or insulated jacket that you are not intending to wear except at camp or on top of Toubkal.

Underwear – you don't need anything specialist but make sure it's comfy.

High-factor sun cream – you'll be walking in a high UV area in summer; factor 50 is the best and lots of it!

Sunglasses – if you're going to spend any money, spend it on a pair of category 3 or 4 sunglasses. These are mountain sunglasses, designed for when spending prolonged time in very high light exposures. Eyes are easy to damage and hard to replace – I wish someone had told me this before my first trip to the high mountains! A

Summer boots and rucksack discarded after the day's trek

slight wind can pick up a lot of dust, so they act as good protection from that too.

Sun hat or head protection – either a cap or full-brimmed sun hat can also help you see against the bright sun. The hood of a sun hoody provides UV protection but doesn't block glare.

Water container – at least 2 litres of capacity. You may need even more if you are completing the Toubkal Circuit. In the high mountains you will have to be able to last the whole day without refilling, and uphill is hot work in the sun.

Sterilisation tablets or water filter – some bottles come with filters built in. Most groups use bottled water, but you can purify tap water or use mountain streams.

Food – some snacks from home would be a good idea if you are a grazer, and some sweets for a little boost halfway up the big peaks. Make sure your snacks aren't the melting variety. For the Toubkal Circuit or longer mountain days, this is particularly worthwhile.

Waterproofs – very useful in shoulder seasons but not likely to be used at the start of summer. That said, July and August can have storms so it's best to pack a waterproof jacket just in case, even if it's only lightweight. It makes a very effective windproof layer on summits at the least. Waterproof trousers are unnecessary in true summer.

Gloves and warm hat – a pair of gloves and something to keep your head warm on Toubkal and on windy summits or during early morning starts.

Sleeping bags or quilts – a summer sleeping bag rated down to 0°C should be adequate for camping and staying in refuges. On some nights indoors, just a sleeping bag liner would be enough. Sometimes sleeping bags can be hired or provided by trekking companies.

Clothes to sleep in – something cool and easy to pack

Camp sandals (optional) – when trekking, if you don't want to keep your boots on all day, you'll need something to walk around in. The same applies for staying in refuges and gîtes. It's more comfortable to have a change of shoes to allow your feet to breathe, and no one wants to wear boots around Marrakech when it's over 30°C. Something like flip-flops, sandals or barefoot shoes would be a good idea: light and easily flattened.

Head torch – despite the long hours of daylight, you will need one for camping and early starts. They are also very useful when the electricity in the refuge turns off unexpectedly. If it isn't rechargeable, bring spare batteries.

Powerpack – there are power sockets in most accommodation but power isn't always available in the refuges, and there is high competition for the small number of sockets (a charger with multiple USB ports goes a long way). On the Toubkal Circuit you will need to be self-sufficient for at least a couple of days at a time.

Trekking poles (optional) – If you prefer to walk with poles or would appreciate the extra balance, bring them. There will be some steep ascents and descents as well as loose ground. You can buy a cheap pair in Imlil or often rent them from a trekking company.

Hand sanitiser or wipes – for before meals and when using toilets, etc. See the 'Health and hygiene' section for more details.

First aid kit – a small personal first aid kit, or group one, is useful for treating minor ailments/injuries (see the 'Accidents and first aid' section of the guidebook).

Entertainment – on the Toubkal Circuit in particular, you will have long afternoons at your campsite in the middle of nowhere. A few card games, or other forms of entertainment, within your group can make a huge difference as to how much you enjoy the trip. It stops you from descending into a monotony of walking, eating and sleeping.

Reaching the top of Ikhibi Nord (Route 10)

ROUTE 7

Imlil Cascades hike

Start/Finish	Imlil's main car park
Duration	1hr to second waterfall
Distance	3km (2 miles)
Ascent	300m (990ft)
Descent	300m (990ft) (returning via ascent route)

Many paths and trails lie between Imlil and the nearby villages of the Mizane Valley, hidden beneath the canopies of walnut trees. Some groups head straight to the start of the Toubkal Trail by Aremd. Others strike out east along the road to begin the Toubkal Circuit. But if you are spending a night in Imlil and have time to explore, here are some suggestions for your rambles. Going for a little wander will help with your acclimatisation, even if you don't fancy a proper hike.

There are many variations within these routes. The main feature is the Imlil Cascades. These waterfalls are a small tourist destination in their own right, with many day-trippers coming to see them. You can expect it to be busy in the middle of the day. I've also added a second waterfall you might like to see as an excuse to extend your walk. The panoramic view out over Imlil is worth the hike even if the waterfall is running quite dry. Equally, if you want views and don't care too much for waterfalls, you could circumnavigate the head of the valley by simply following the road.

From Imlil's main car park at the northernmost entrance to the valley, walk uphill along the main street, past **shops** on either side of the road: cafés, bakeries, second-hand outdoor gear. At the first fork in the road, take the right-hand bend and continue to walk slightly uphill along another shopping street. At the end of this short street, turn left (again, uphill) on the road. You should see the switchbacks in the road above you as it winds up the hillside. On the very first corner of those switchbacks, don't turn but instead continue straight on down a narrow footpath. There are a couple more shops on the right and you might have to squeeze between some high vegetation but continue on that footpath.

The path comes out in an open area of stony, dusty hillside under a high canopy of walnut trees. You should see a zigzagging path ahead of you, with some

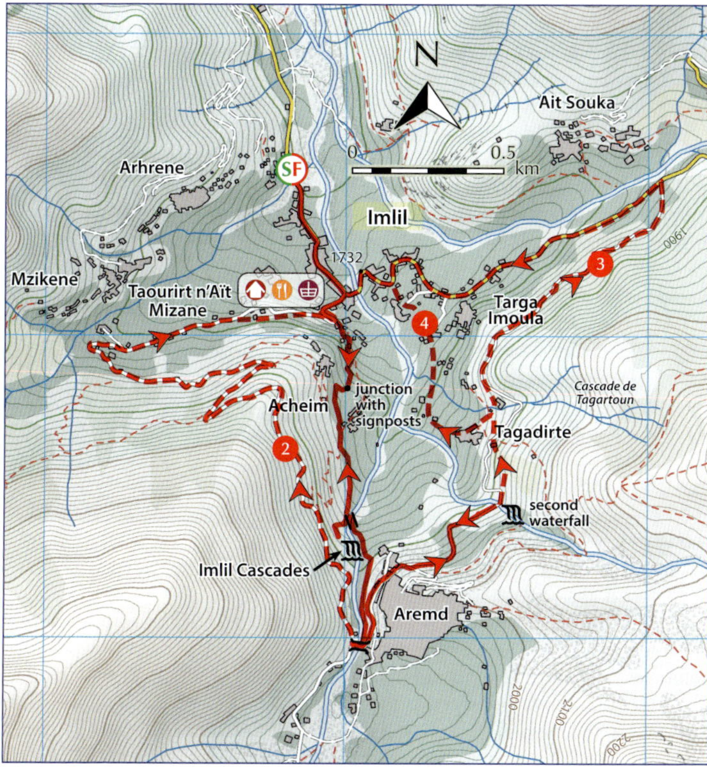

shallow steps slowly winding upwards. There is a bit of a stream on the left and in front of you should be a low stone wall. Follow the winding path until it meets this wall and turns right to pass alongside, reaching a **junction with signposts** to several different gîtes and dars.

Go left, following that same wall for a little longer and continuing along the dusty track. You will likely pass more stalls selling tourist goods, like jewellery and geodes, laid out on carpets. Keep going until you reach the *saqia* (leat). This is a water irrigation channel, one of many used to move fresh water around the villages. Follow along the side of this narrow channel – whichever side looks easiest to you. There are a few small bridges but it is easy to step across to the other side if needed. As this is the edge of the treeline, you might get a glimpse of the mountains beyond in the far distance. Keep going until you see a gorge emerging ahead. As you reach the mouth of the gorge, you will see a river with lots of little wooden ladders laid out between boulders, like bridges. In winter, these **bridges** are necessary to cross the river, but in summer there may be very little water and you can cross by stepping across the boulders.

Imlil Cascades

At the back of this gorge, just around the corner from the bridges, is the first waterfall of the walk. These are known as the **Imlil Cascades**, and you'll see it is a veritable tourist site. The narrow space is crammed with café tables and orange juice stands – and local entrepreneurs trying to sell you jewellery. It's hard to loiter without getting swept up into a café or into making a purchase. But you can get down to the foot of the waterfall by squeezing past all the tables.

When you are done, retrace your steps to the large boulder at the mouth of the gorge. You arrived here on the path from the left, so instead take the path that continues right and steeply uphill in a series of steps. Again, it might be hard to stop here, but the view out across the valley is rather nice. Climb up the steep stone steps and beyond, following the path over tree roots. Go directly past a building – keeping just to its left – and continue up, past another saqia on your left, and up again… until you eventually pop out of the trees on a wide dirt track. Go right and downhill a little, following the track above the river until you hit the road just as it crosses a large bridge over the river. You should see the distinctive sharp corners of the road on the far bank as it zigzags down to the bridge.

From the bridge, do not cross but instead turn left – away from the river – following the road towards the village of **Aremd**, gaining height on the hillside. Continue through the village, sticking to the road until, beyond the buildings, you come to a clear Y-junction. One road continues up and right towards the hillside. The other drops down over a little hump and curves left and down, almost contouring as it continues into a grove of trees. Take the left-hand, lower road. As you do, the views really open up and you can see back down across Imlil and the wider valley. Ahead, the hillside opposite is strewn with huge boulders. Stay on this road and follow it through the grove of trees and around the bend to the **second waterfall**.

This waterfall is the river **Assif n'Imserdane**. It may not have much water if the weather is very dry. If you continue along the road a bit further, to where it curves around the nose of the hillside, and look back it is much more impressive.

Options for return

1 Feeling hot and bothered: retrace your steps all the way back (this route in reverse) mostly in the shade of the walnut trees. It is quicker than the climb as it is mainly downhill and you know the path.

2 Short and no navigation: from the second waterfall, retrace your steps down the road to the bridge over the main river. Cross the bridge and follow the road all the way around the west side of the valley and down the switchbacks. It will take you back to the end of the second shopping street you walked up at the start of the walk.

3 Long and no navigation: stay on the road that contours around the bowl of the valley on the eastern side, with views out across Imlil. Continue towards Ait Souka. At the road junction, turn left and follow the road down to Imlil. This is much longer than retracing your steps to the bridge and going the other way around the valley.

4 More exploration: there is a way to cut the corner and return to the starting point on a different path down through the walnut trees. However, although it is marked on most maps, the way is not at all obvious. It's a maze of faint dirt tracks that pass a carpet shop and then continue along a saqia. It is marked on the map and GPX files are provided – good luck!

Path above the river, looking south

ROUTE 8

Imlil to Base Camp

Start	Toubkal trailhead
Finish	Base Camp
Duration	4½–5hr
Distance	9km (5½ miles)
Ascent	1300m (4270ft)
Descent	0m
Warning	You cannot start up this trail later than 3pm.

The first step to climbing Toubkal is the hike from Imlil to Toubkal Base Camp, where the two refuges are sited at 3200m. You'll set out from wherever you stayed overnight in and around Imlil or Aremd. Or if you didn't spend a night, you may be driven to the trailhead or hike up from the centre of Imlil. (Use the map from 'Route 7 – Imlil Cascades hike' if need be.) Since there are many ways to do this, we'll start from the trailhead. The hike from there is almost entirely uphill, not all steep but persistent none the less. There will be plenty of cafés along the way; the ones at Sidi Chamharouch have a toilet.

There is no particular marking or sign for the trailhead. Start from the highest road bridge that crosses over the river from Aremd. Looking south, across the stony plain to the mountains in the distance, you should be able to see the trail you'll be taking. Cross to the west side of the bridge and turn left up the road past a few buildings.

At the corner of the road, take the footpath that bears left between the two stone-walled enclosures and out across the plain. The enclosures are filled with fruit trees. Cross the alluvial plain: the flat, barren landscape created by the river. It is very stony underfoot and the dust can really whip up in the wind. The trail bears left across the wide-open area then zigzags up the left-hand side of the valley towards a big building. This is a police checkpoint and it will be manned even if you don't have to go inside.

Beyond this, the path contours the left-hand side of the valley, slowly rising. The path is quite wide, making a nice flat ledge to walk on above the steep slope down to the river below. There are many small stalls and stick-roofed cafés along the way selling Toubkal souvenirs or drinks: mint tea, freshly squeezed orange

Map continues on page 94

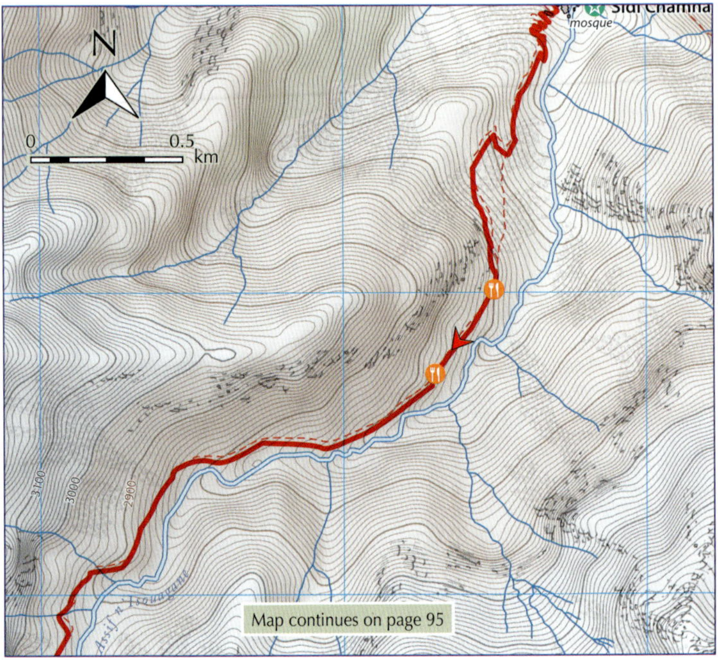

juice and bottled lemonades. The path winds in and out of the curves of the hillside until you arrive at **Sidi Chamharouch**.

This is the site of a shrine and small mosque for pilgrims. All around this bend in the valley are more cafés and stalls. This is also your last chance to use a toilet before reaching the refuges. Cross the bridge over the river that cascades down from the mountains right next to the bridge. Then hike up the path's tight zigzags to regain height, this time on the right-hand slope of the valley.

The tomb of **Sidi Chamharouch** is said to lie beneath the white-painted boulder beside the trail to Toubkal Base Camp. Sidi Chamharouch is the King of the Djinn or Lord of Demons, and it is said he will grant wishes if you bring him gifts and offerings. The waters that flow from the hillside are said to cure ailments. This is a popular pilgrimage site and no tourists are allowed to visit. The site was worshipped pre-Islam and a mosque was built next to the boulder when Islam came to Morocco.

View back down over the river towards Imlil

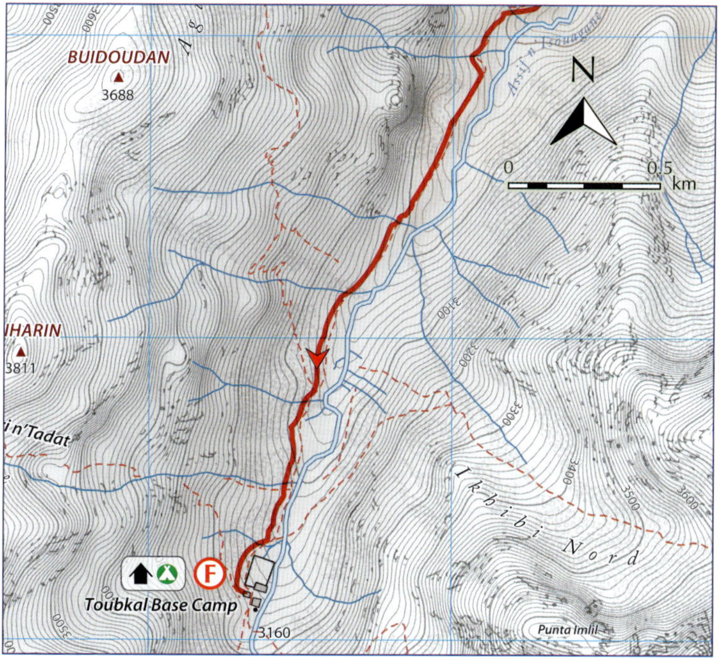

Looking back, you should be able to clearly see the white-painted boulder that marks the shrine. Now continue on into the mountains, where boulders and crags gradually start to replace the small trees that dot the slopes. Walk along the ledge below some grand cliff faces. Again, the path is wide and flat underfoot as this is the main thoroughfare into the mountains for hikers and mules. The route passes by two more small cafés before the long final climb to the refuges. This last section is much flatter as the valley opens out into a wide bowl and soon the welcome sight of the refuges.

TOUBKAL BASE CAMP

Two refuges now stand in the valley west of Toubkal. The lower refuge is Les Mouflons. The upper, with its distinctive tower, is CAF Toubkal. The open-fronted building to the right is the remains of the Neltner refuge, which was in use between 1938 and 1999. Beyond this is the green-roofed police check-point. If you stand outside either of these refuges and face north, you'll be looking back at the same mountains that stand above Imlil and Tacheddirt, although Imlil itself is out of sight. To the west are the formidable flanks of Biguinoussene. As you look south and up the valley, you'll see Tizi n'Ouagane, although you can't see the top. And to the east lies Toubkal. You cannot see the summit, but Ikhibi Sud is the hanging valley directly behind the refuges.

Arriving at Toubkal Base Camp

ROUTE 9

Base Camp to Toubkal summit (normal – Ikhibi Sud)

Start/Finish	Base Camp
Duration	6hr; to Toubkal summit 4–5hr
Distance	3.5km (2¼ miles)
Ascent	1100m (3610ft)
Descent	1100m (3610ft) (returning via ascent route)

The ascent of Toubkal via the most common (normal) route is through the south cwm, Ikhibi Sud. The route can be split into three distinct parts: the initial ascent from Base Camp to the cwm, the crossing of the cwm to reach the ridge at Tizi n'Toubkal and finally the climb along the ridge to reach Toubkal's summit. Most groups set off in the dark (at 3–4am) to reach the top during or just after sunrise. This is also to avoid climbing in the heat of the day and to allow time for the groups descending back to Imlil the same day.

WALKING IN THE DARK

For many this will be their first time hiking in the dark, never mind climbing a mountain above 4000m. Make sure your head torch works and is fully charged the night before. Our eyes are adapted to see better out of the corners than the middle at night. This is due to the concentration of light receptors for colour vs black and white, so looking side on at something can make it clearer. It takes about 20 minutes for your eyes to adjust to the darkness after being in a lit room. Also be aware that your depth perception will be worse in the dark.

The path starts down the paved corridor between the two refuges, with steps down towards the river. Cross the river here on stepping stones, it should be very low in midsummer, and take the path that continues out from it, beginning the uphill. After a short initial section going right, the route swings back left and traverses the convex slope below Ikhibi Sud. In the darkness, you'll see the strings of lights moving on the mountain above and behind you – lines of head torches making their way towards Toubkal.

The path continues up through a group of large boulders. You'll have to squeeze between two to get by and then turn right to start the next traverse.

TINHARIN
3811
3744
Tizi n'Tadat
Toubkal Base Camp
3160
edge of cwm
N
0
0.5
km
Ikhibi Nord
Ikhibi Sud
Punta Imlil
TIBHERINE
3887
Tizi n'Ouanas
IMOUZZER
4010
North Col
TOUBKAL
4167
Aiguille d'Ifni
SE Ridge
Col d'Ifni
3756
Tizi n'Imouzzer
Tete D'Ouanoums
3970
TOUBKAL W.
4030
Tizi n'Toubkal
Jebel Toubkal
Ouanoums Ridge
3658
Tizi n'Ouanoums
Assif Bou Tiouna

Sunrise starts on the slopes behind

There's a slab of rock you have to walk across too here. Some boulders overhang, so make sure you're looking up and not just at the ground. This section takes you to the next corner in the path, on the lip of **Ikhibi Sud**.

Continue up the footpath along the right edge of Ikhibi Sud. To your right are the slopes of Toubkal West and to the left the distinctive point of Punta Imlil. Towards the back of the cwm, you'll round the corner to the right, heading up the screes to the pass of **Tizi n'Toubkal**. As you climb, remember to look back at the view behind you, where the opposite ridge will be bathed in warm light. The distinctive lump in the centre is called the Clochetons.

Reaching Tizi n'Toubkal, you are most of the way to the summit. This is nearly 4000m above sea level, so you may be feeling the altitude by now. To the west is the sharp edge connecting to Toubkal West. To the east is a broader ridgeline; head in this direction. As you approach the nose of the ridge, look out for the window between rocks that frames the summit of Toubkal and its distinctive black metal pyramid. You're nearly there.

Head up the ridge. It's not sharp and there is a path almost the whole way. It's safer to stay on the left-hand side, well away from the sheer drop to the right – in case you stumble. Unlike in winter, this section does not feel particularly exposed, so continue on up until you step out onto the summit plateau. The summit pyramid should immediately come into view on your right. Turn the corner, still following the path, and reach the summit.

The summit of Toubkal is marked by a distinctive, square-based **black metal pyramid**, which stands several metres high. It was built in 1931 as a triangulation point.

The summit marker is close to the southernmost edge of Toubkal, with a sheer drop. Views look out south in a wide east-to-west panorama, covering all the eastern peaks of Toubkal National Park and beyond to the Anti-Atlas and Jbel Sirwa. Dome d'Ifni is directly below, and you can even see as far as the Sahara on a clear day.

Descent options

Most people descend by retracing their steps to Toubkal Base Camp (**2hr**).

It is possible to take in the summit of Toubkal West on this descent if you have the time (add **30–45min** to descent time): from Tizi n'Toubkal, continue along the ridgeline ahead of you – with a small section of slightly exposed scrambling. Then take the footpath through the screes to rejoin the path down Ikhibi Sud, near the top.

Alternatively, you could descend via the north cwm, Ikhibi Nord (**2½hr**). Follow the directions for the Route 10 Ikhibi Nord ascent route in reverse or the Route 11 full horseshoe route.

Toubkal summit; photo by Alex Roddie

ROUTE 10

Base Camp to Toubkal summit (alternative – Ikhibi Nord)

Start/Finish	Base Camp
Duration	7hr; to Toubkal summit 4½–5hr
Distance	4km (2½ miles)
Ascent	1100m (3610ft)
Descent	1100m (3610ft) (returning via ascent route)

An alternative way to climb Toubkal is via the north cwm, Ikhibi Nord. This is a steeper and longer route, but it avoids the crowds of people climbing and descending on Ikhibi Sud. You must walk downhill from Base Camp to access the cwm. After that, the climb is a fairly constant ascent until about 3850m, below the peak of Tibherine. Here the route follows a shallow section across the North Col before turning right and completing the short scrambly section onto Toubkal's summit plateau. Due to the easy scrambling, steepness and length, it is slightly more difficult than the normal route.

North side of Toubkal lit by sunrise

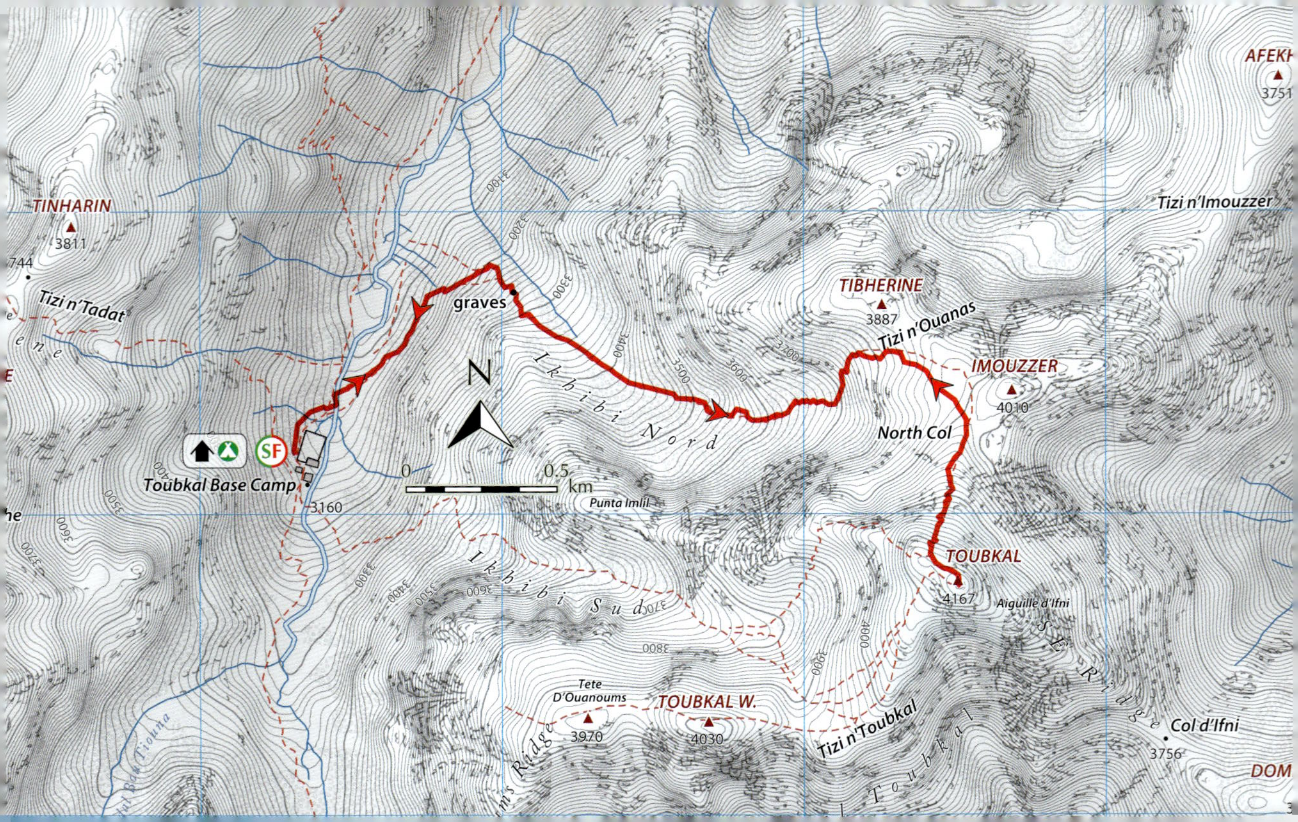

TINHARIN
3811
Tizi n'Tadat
Toubkal Base Camp
SF
3160
graves
N
0
0.5
km
Punta Imlil
Ikhibi Nord
Ikhibi Sud
TIBHERINE
3887
Tizi n'Ouanas
IMOUZZER
4010
North Col
TOUBKAL
4167
Aiguille d'Ifni
S.E. Ridge
Col d'Ifni
3756
Tizi n'Imouzzer
AFEK
3751
Tete D'Ouanoums
3970
TOUBKAL W.
4030
Tizi n'Toubkal
DOM
3100
3200
3300
3400
3500
3600
3700
3800
3900
4000

From the refuges, head downhill past the terraces on the main Sidi Chamharouch path. After not very long at all, another path will branch off right – almost doubling back – towards the river. Take it and cross the **river** onto its eastern bank. Climb up the bank onto the path above it that runs parallel to the river, gaining height on the nose of the ridge that descends from the right.

Once you are on the top of this broad ridge, turn right and uphill along it. This will lead you towards the start of Ikhibi Nord. Ahead you should see a cluster of large boulders. As you approach the first big boulder, stop and look down. Just in front of this boulder, some 10–20m downhill, is a line of **unmarked graves**. They're very easy to miss – if you set out in the dark you won't even see them. This is the resting place of the crew and passengers from a plane crash in 1969.

PLANE CRASH ON TIBHERINE

In December 1969, a Lockheed L-749 Constellation aircraft crashed into Tibherine. It was flying from Portugal to the Republic of Biafra with three crew members and five passengers, transporting ammunition for the civil war. The plane lost height due to engine failure and struck the mountain. The bodies that were found were buried at the lip of the cwm. Due to the rocky terrain, the graves are like stone boxes sunk into the ground, with flat slabs of rock placed over the tops. These slabs have gaps between them so be warned – you might see bones if you look too closely.

Continue up towards the boulders. The path is a little less obvious through them – again, harder in the dark – and there are some small cairns marking the way but they are easily missed. Keep on the path as it exits the boulders and start the long steep climb up **Ikhibi Nord**.

The path, despite making a clearly visible line across the scree, is loose underfoot – especially in the steeper sections near the top of the cwm. On your way, look out for the numerous pieces of metal littered across the screes to your left. These are all parts of the crashed plane – fuselage, control panel, window…

PLANE CRASH DEBRIS

The plane seems to have hit the exact summit of Tibherine. Part of the engine has become the summit marker for Tibherine. The rest of the aircraft is scattered down Ikhibi Nord – and presumably on the other side of Tibherine too, if one could get there. Some of these pieces have moved further down the mountain since the 2023 earthquake.

In his book *The High Atlas*, Hamish Brown writes, 'I actually descended to it from Toubkal out of curiosity as the peak glittered – with what proved to be thousands of rounds of ammunition, exploded or otherwise. The engine reeked of oil… They said all hell broke loose after I'd gone – police, army, the lot, looking for a crashed plane.'

Tibherine's summit cairn

As you climb, you should see a short cliff ahead of you. To pass this, follow the path to just below it and then bear left along the base of it. The path then turns east again and, climbing steeply up for a short section, you will step out of the cwm onto flatter ground that leads to the North Col. The peak to the left is Tibherine, the one straight ahead is Imouzzer.

To continue to Toubkal, cross the shallow slope on the path that cuts across to the right of Imouzzer. This is the true **North Col**. The ridge up to the right, due south, is the way to Toubkal. This last section of ridge is a little scrambly – you will find it helpful to use your hands. The fins of rock that stick out of the ground are sound and grippy, but the ground itself is quite loose. Although short, it can feel quite airy in the middle, with a long drop down on the left.

Finally, step off the ridge onto the summit plateau of **Toubkal**. The famous black metal pyramid will be at the opposite end of the plateau; follow the faint path through the small piles of stones to reach it.

Descend the way you came (**2½hr**) or, more usually, take the shorter Ikhibi South route (**2hr**) back to the refuges.

ROUTE 11

Full Toubkal horseshoe

Start/Finish	Base Camp
Duration	7–8hr
Distance	9km (5½ miles)
Ascent	1300m (4270ft)
Descent	1300m (4270ft)

For those feeling energetic, it is possible to complete a full horseshoe of peaks while also taking in Toubkal. This involves starting up Ikhibi Sud, splitting off to climb Toubkal West, then rejoining the usual south cwm route to reach Toubkal. You then descend via the North Col, splitting off to take in Imouzzer and Tibherine before finishing the descent down the usual Ikhibi Nord route. This is a big day but a very rewarding one. It can be done in either direction but anticlockwise is more common and allows you to see the interesting historical points of Ikhibi Nord in daylight.

You can refer to the two ascent routes for more detail but in brief, set out from the refuges along the usual Ikhibi Sud route. As you reach the top of the cwm, but before Tizi n'Toubkal is in sight, a path splits off from the main path to your right. Take this up the north-facing scree slopes of **Toubkal West** to reach its summit. Turn east and walk along the ridgeline to **Tizi n'Toubkal**. The path is just below the ridge, on its north side.

From the col, continue as per usual up to the summit of **Toubkal** then cross the plateau to find the north ridge that descends to the **North Col**. This is the hardest navigation of the day, as there are steep cliffs all around and you will not see the ridge until you are standing above it. This short ridge descent involves a little down scrambling. It is good, grippy rock but everything else is very loose underfoot and a slide to the right would have serious consequences. Take it slow and steady.

At the bottom of the ridge, take the upper path across the col and cut off right as the slope of Imouzzer presents itself. There are two summits to **Imouzzer** and the first is marked by a small cairn. The second is separated from the first by a 5m-deep gully that is not passable for hikers.

From Imouzzer, cut across right to rejoin the upper path and follow it around the top of the bowl towards Tibherine. There are a couple of steps of scrambling to reach the very top. The summit of **Tibherine** is marked by the hunk of twisted

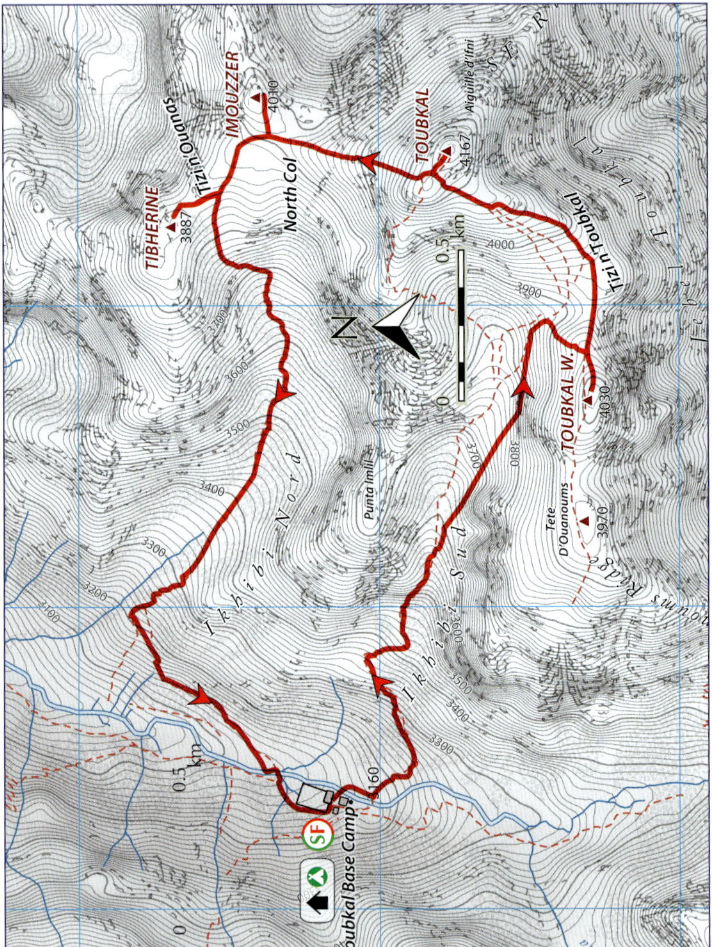

aircraft engine securely balanced on the right of the north edge of the peak, above a dizzying drop. Descend Tibherine's south-east slope to rejoin the path at the top edge of Ikhibi Nord. Then descend the usual route back to the refuge.

Imouzzer summit, looking north-west

ROUTE 12

Ouanoukrim

Start/Finish	Base Camp
Duration	6–7hr
Distance	8.5km (5¼ miles)
Ascent	1100m (3610ft)
Descent	1100m (3610ft)
Warning	Ridge scramble, not to be attempted in high winds. In low visibility, it can be difficult to refind the start of the scramble on descent.

Ouanoukrim is the second-highest mountain in the High Atlas after Toubkal. It has two peaks: Ras (4083m) and Timesguida (4089m). It is situated due south of Toubkal, at the end of the line of mountains on the opposite side of the valley. To reach the two summits involves a short section of scrambling along the east ridge, but most of the ascent is done in reaching the pass below it, Tizi n'Ouagane. The summits themselves are on easy-angled terrain, with Ras being the steeper. This route takes in both peaks, Timesguida first then Ras, but it can just as easily be done in reverse.

From Toubkal Base Camp, walk south, slowly ascending the valley on the path that runs along the right-hand side. Keep going past the cliffs of Afella and the band of yellow crags on your right. Beyond this, the path stays right and traverses below the east face of Akioud, zigzagging up through the scree as the ground steepens. It is a little looser underfoot here. The distinctive notch in the ridgeline out to the left is Tizi n'Ouanoums. The cliffs above you are the start of Ouanoukrim. Continue uphill, until you reach the pass of **Tizi n'Ouagane**, with views south towards the Anti-Atlas and back the way you've come. The isolated peak east of the pass is Bou Ouzzal.

Overlooking Ouanoukrim's east ridge, the little summit of **Bou Ouzzal** is sadly often ignored, since it is only 3860m. That said, it is not very far from the pass if you have the time and inclination to take it in. The southernmost summit is the highest point and you can see a path from the pass.

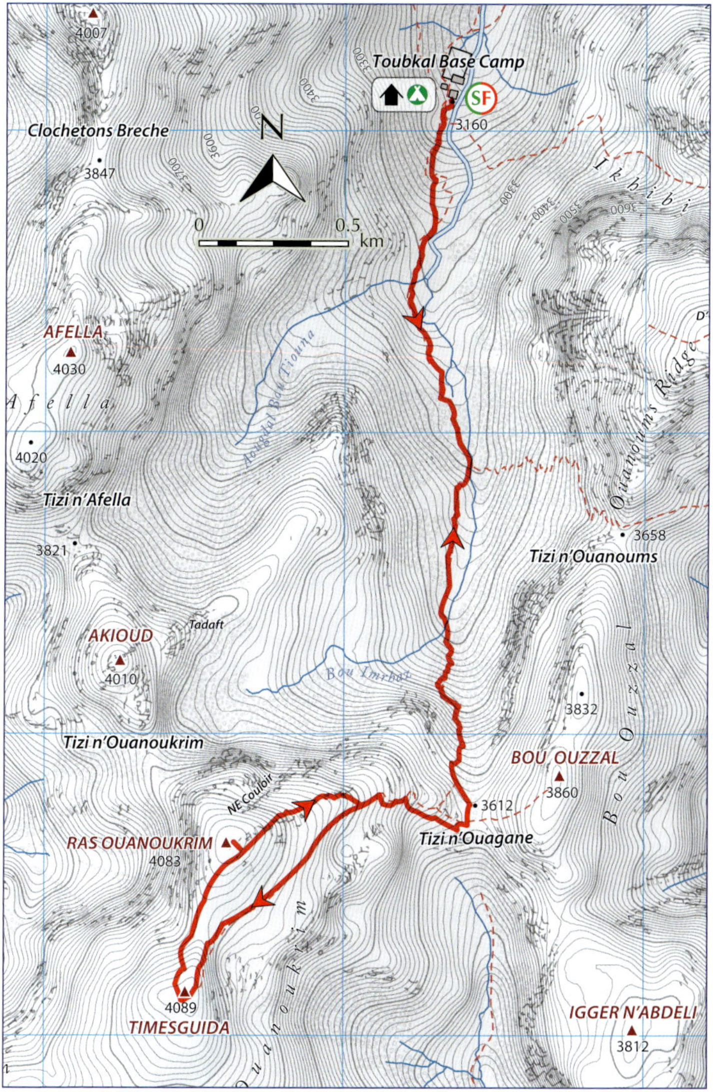

Toubkal Base Camp
SF
3160
Clochetons Breche
3847
4007
0
0.5
km
AFELLA
4030
Afella
4020
Tizi n'Afella
3821
Aoughal Bou Tiouna
Ikhibi
Ouanoums Ridge
3658
Tizi n'Ouanoums
Tadaft
AKIOUD
4010
Bou Imrhaz
3832
Tizi n'Ouanoukrim
BOU OUZZAL
3860
NE Couloir
3612
Tizi n'Ouagane
RAS OUANOUKRIM
4083
Bou Ouzzal
Ouanoukrim
4089
TIMESGUIDA
IGGER N'ABDELI
3812

Ras from near the summit of Timesguida

To get onto Ouanoukrim's massif from Tizi n'Ouagane, there is a short section of straightforward but unavoidable scrambling. You cannot walk around the scramble. It is no more than about 100m in length but has sheer drops on either side and should not be attempted in high winds. Note that this is the gateway to the mountain; you must do in reverse whatever you do to ascend.

From the pass, head west up the initial slope presented to you. Ahead you should see two pinnacles of rock some 5–7m tall. Pass these fingers on the right, with a short descent and then ascent, moving back towards the left to cross behind them and regain the ridge. Scramble upwards, heading slightly right, sticking to the middle of the ridge. There are a couple of sections to scramble but the rock has good grip and plenty of handholds. Keep climbing, following the right-hand edge of the mountain as it veers off – but at a safe distance – until the ground flattens.

You should see a scree slope up ahead with a path cutting off left and across the slope. Take this path and follow it on a gentle uphill ascent to **Timesguida**. This peak has a plateau summit without a clear highest point, but there are several stacks of rocks and a small drystone wall shelter to mark the top. From here you can see across to the back of Akioud, Afella's south summit and on the far left, the flat top of Tazaghart.

The huge **Tazaghart Plateau** (3980m) is about 3km² and is popular with ski tourers. Its high point is Talat n'Ifri, on the right-hand end of the summit from this viewpoint. Its north face has many ridges and gullies.

Behind you (due north) is the inviting, easy-angled slope across to Ras, the triangular second summit. Take the path beyond the cairn and through the screes down one slope and back up the other side. Of the two tops visible, you should be aiming for the right-hand one first. Once there, cross the tiny arête at the top of the steep gully (Ouanoukrim's central couloir) and scramble up to the true summit of **Ras**. This feels airy as you cross, even if it's only a few steps. The small top of Ras Ouanoukrim sits high above the Toubkal valley, isolated by steepness on all sides. Look for the small rock with the summit's name and height to prove you're at the top.

When you're ready, cross back over the arête onto the lower summit. Follow the zigzagging path due east down the scree slope back towards the scramble. If in doubt, veer right (away from the edge) until you cross the path you took to Timesguida. Downclimb the scramble, this time passing to the left of the pinnacles, to reach **Tizi n'Ouagane**. Then retrace your steps to the refuge.

Descending back into the valley

ROUTE 13

Aguelzim

Start/Finish	Base Camp
Duration	4–5hr
Distance	9km (5½ miles)
Ascent	1000m (3280ft)
Descent	1000m (3280ft)

Despite not making the 4000m cut off, Aguelzim (3663m) is a very worthy mountain in its own right. It has a mule track almost all the way up it, making for a straightforward ascent and swooping descent back to the refuges. You can enjoy the view without having to think too much about your feet. The short section off route is pleasant and is an excellent vantage point for viewing both of Toubkal's main ascent routes. In fact, these are the best views of the Toubkal Massif that a hiker can get. If you don't want to climb the full mountain, an excursion up the path for a view back down across the valley is well worth it.

From the refuges, head roughly south down the Sidi Chamharouch path. On the left, just past the wall corner that encloses the terraced camping area, a broad track splits off uphill. Take this path and follow it as it traverses uphill on a gentle incline through the scree. As you climb, more and more lumpy crags and boulders appear on the slopes above and below. There is only one path here, so just keep going.

Eventually, the path turns a bend around the corner of the mountain above, where the switchbacks start. Pause for a minute here and take in the best viewpoint over the Mizane Valley. You can see Imlil in the valley bottom and all the way across to Toubkal and Ouanoukrim. Both of the routes up Ikhibi Nord and Ikhibi Sud are visible, and even the tiny triangle marking the summit can be spotted on a clear day.

To continue, head up the path as it bends right around the side of **Aguelzim** to the pass. Take note of this last point where the path crosses the ridge; this is the point you'll come down to after descending the ridgeline above you. If you prefer to scramble up this sort of bouldery ground rather than descend, then do this next section of the route in reverse.

AGUELZIM NORTH
3553
3416
3521
Tizi n'Aguelzim
AGUELZIM SOUTH
3663
Aguelzim
BUIDOUDAN
3688
TINHARIN
3811
n'Tadat
3744
Tizi n'Tadat
Pinnacle
BIGUINNOUSSENE
4007
Clochetons Breche
3847
Toubkal Base Camp
3160
Punta Imlil
Ikhibi Nord
Ikhibi Sud
Assif n'Isougane
0
0.5
km
N
SF

Aguelzim's summit marker

Otherwise, continue up the mule path to the col of **Tizi n'Aguelzim**. This route is for the higher south summit but, if you wanted to, you could turn right at the pass, follow the top of the broad ridge up to Aguelzim North then return to the pass. For the true summit, turn left as you reach the pass and make your way uphill along the crest. There is a bit of a path in places but you are really finding your own way up the broad slope to the top. A wooden board marks the south summit of **Aguelzim**.

The views east are still good, though cut off by the mountain you're standing on. But to the south you can see towards Biguinoussene, and south-west gives a clear view of the north face of the Tazaghart Plateau with its many folds and gullies. Again, if you wanted to, you could extend the hike by continuing along the easy-angled ridge to the next peak due south, Buidoudan (3688m), which you can see just across the way.

Descending Aguelzim's east spur

From Aguelzim South summit, descend the east ridge. This is steep and lumpy, without being actual scrambling, but it has incredible views across to Tichki and its west facing crags. This descent is fairly steep and there is no path. If you decide it doesn't look good – perhaps the wind has picked up – then simply retrace your steps to the path at Tizi n'Aguelzim.

Back on the mule track again, retrace your steps down to the viewpoint and then continue all the way back to the refuges. Enjoy the views.

Although the heights of the peaks in this area are not consistent across the various maps, it's generally agreed that there are seven mountain summits in Toubkal National Park above 4000m:

1 Toubkal (4167m)
2 Ouanoukrim's two peaks: Ras (4083m) and Timesguida (4089m)
3 Toubkal West (4030m)
4 Afella's two peaks: North (roughly 4030m) and South (4020m)
5 Akioud (4010m)
6 Imouzzer (4010m)
7 Biguinoussene (4007m)

Of course, there are many other excellent peaks that are just shy of 4000m and are therefore forgotten, simply because of a few metres (e.g. Aguelzim and Tibherine). Out of this list of 4000ers, we have already covered Toubkal, Ouanoukrim, Toubkal West and Imouzzer. I will briefly cover the others for completeness, since a few of you are undoubtedly wondering…

Akioud

To climb Akioud, start up the valley from the Toubkal refuges, heading due south along the right-hand side of the river. A stream runs out of the gorge to the right of the path; cross it and turn immediately right as though to follow the stream uphill. A faint path with occasional cairns leads you to the right-hand end of the distinctive yellowish crag above. Scramble up over a series of short rock steps to reach the top. Beyond is a clearer path and the bowl of a cwm, with Akioud at the back and the craggy flanks of Afella rising high to the right. Something of a path initially leads you up into the scree fields at the back of the valley. From here you will be climbing without a path on increasingly loose and steep scree… scrabbling along upwards while the ground beneath you tries to slide down again. When you reach the pass (right of the headwall), after another short scramble, Akioud is up on your left. The path here is more solid again, taking you below a sheer rock wall on your left, with a short final scramble to the summit. Return the way you came. Helmets are recommended for rockfall.

Afella

Afella is a lovely mountain but horrible to access for a hiker. From the Toubkal refuges during summer, it involves either a very long hike beyond Tizi n'Afella, which is almost entirely scree swimming, or Grade 3+ scrambling or rock climbing. This is not a beginners' peak and there are no physical paths from the east. Not recommended.

Biguinoussene

Biguinoussene is an imposing broad peak when seen from halfway up Ikhibi Sud, with the Clochetons to its south and the Tadat pinnacle to the north. Again, to reach the true summit requires either involved scrambling or rock climbing. Unfortunately, many maps, including the OAC maps used in this book, mark a path from the Toubkal refuges to Tizi n'Tadat. One look at the slope is enough to convince you that there is no such path. It is more scree swimming between crags, with lots of very steep, loose rock. Again, this is not a recommended peak for summer hikers. Karl Smith in *Trekking in the Atlas Mountains* described it as 'utter misery guaranteed' and it turns out he wasn't exaggerating.

Biguinoussene from the west slope of Afella

TOUBKAL CIRCUIT

Descent path from Tizi n'Ououraine (Toubkal Circuit, Stage 3)

Tacheddirt
2
Tizi n'Tamatert
Imlil
SF
1
Tizi n'Likemt
N
Aksoual
0
2
4
km
3
Azib Likem
Sidi Chamharouch
Adrar n'Tiniline
6
Toubkal
Toubkal
Base Camp
Dome d'Ifni
Tizi n'Ououra
Tizi
n'Ouanoums
5
Lac Ifni
4
Amsouzert

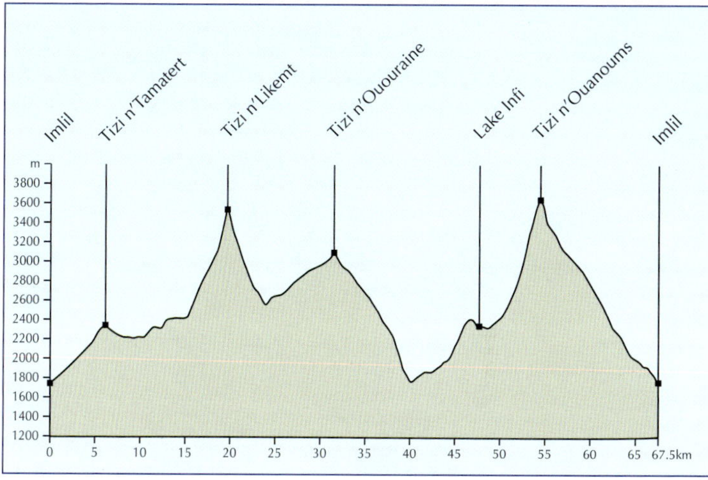

Starting and finishing in Imlil and taking in 5850m of ascent and descent, the Toubkal Circuit is a 67.5km six-day trek in Toubkal National Park. Like many tours in Europe (e.g. the Tour du Mont Blanc), it circles around the Toubkal Massif, taking in several passes – and can be complete in itself without actually summiting Toubkal. Most people do, naturally, add in the ascent of Toubkal on the last day, after spending the night at one of the Toubkal refuges.

Not only is the Toubkal Circuit a great way to gently acclimatise to the altitude but it also provides a real insight into Toubkal National Park: its trails and inhabitants beyond the most popular peaks. You will become immersed in the landscape and culture of these mountains by necessity as you pass through them. If you have the time and inclination to move slowly through the lower valleys, with your eyes and ears open, you will not be disappointed. That said, this is not a well-worn route with smooth trails and ample waymarking. Even compared to the trail up Toubkal, these paths are rough. You will have to spend at least three out of five nights in a tent without access to flushing toilets, a comfortable seat or showers. You will also be expected to get up very early some days – maybe even three or four o'clock in the morning – to get the day's walking done before the afternoon heat. This does mean long, lazy afternoons at camp to recover.

The trails, though rough, are good enough for mules so you'll have help carrying camping equipment and

food, which means you can walk with just a day bag if you choose. You won't have access to anything carried by the mules during the walk, so make sure to have everything you need for the day – especially enough water. Typically, you will leave camp with your guide early, before the mules. The rest of the team will pack up everything and set off after you with the loaded mules. They will overtake you, usually sometime mid-morning, and arrive at camp first. By the time you get there, all the tents will be pitched and food already cooking.

Each day, the general pattern is to get up fairly early, hike up and over the big pass for the day, then descend into the next valley. All timings include a lunch break.

STAGE 1

Imlil to Tacheddirt

Start	Imlil
Finish	Tacheddirt
Duration	4–5hr
Distance	11.5km (7¼ miles)
Ascent	1050m (3440ft)
Descent	400m (1310ft)
High point	Tizi n'Tamatert
Common start time	8am

Today's walk is a simple introduction to trekking in the High Atlas that will ease you into the Toubkal Circuit. The day is straightforward, on good paths with easy terrain underfoot. The route climbs out of Imlil's Mizane Valley, travelling due east into the next valley, over Tizi n'Tamatert. This pass sits just below Tamalaroute (2724m) and can be seen from the windows and balconies of guest houses on the western slopes of Imlil. At only 2299m, this is the lowest pass of the Circuit. Beyond this there is only a little more descent to just outside the village of Tacheddirt. If you are staying in accommodation in Tacheddirt, the day's distance will be a little longer.

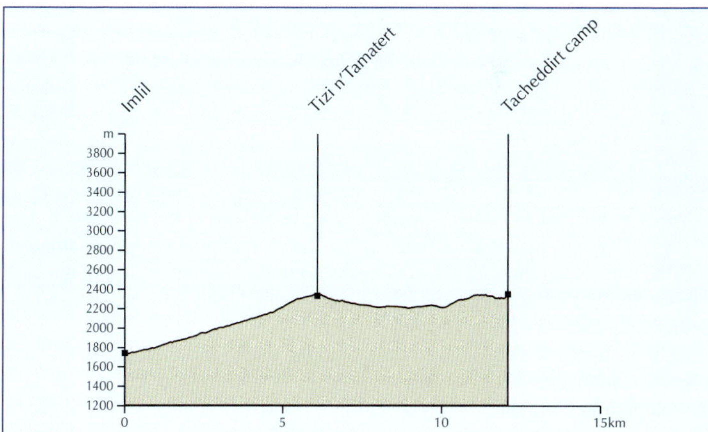

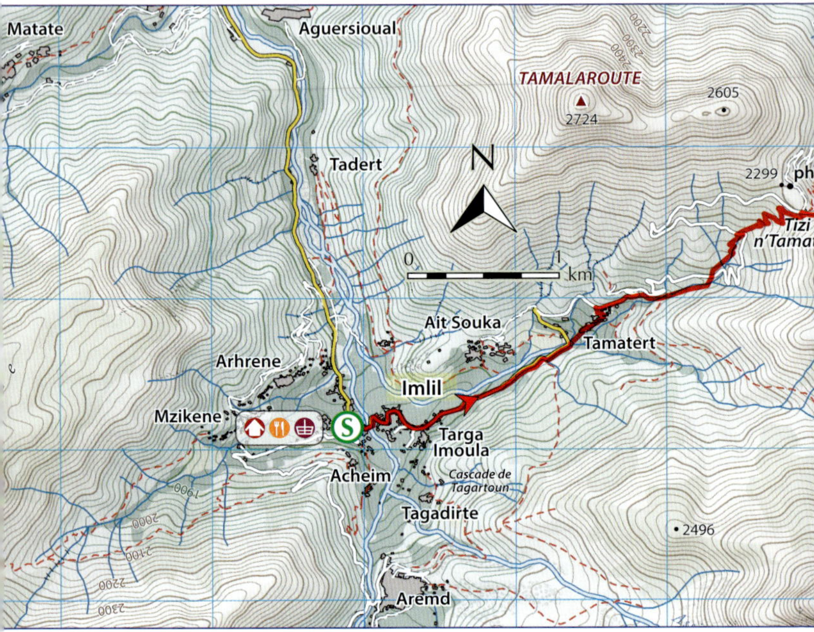

Start from the big car park at the entrance to Imlil. Walk uphill on the road, passing many shops with hiking gear hanging outside (last chance for emergency trekking poles). At the fork, take the left and stay on the main road. Continue uphill, over a bridge and past the last of the shops and guest houses. The road is lined on either side by walnut trees.

As the road bends around to the left, take a right up a footpath on the corner between two drystone walls. The path continues north-east and looks like a cross between a lane and a riverbed. Up some steps at the end of the path, you'll pass by the old kasbah – a sort of fortified house – and through the village of **Tamatert**. Looking back down the valley, you can now see Imlil looking like it is in the middle of a forest of walnut trees. The pass directly behind Imlil is Tizi n'Mzik and the prominent peak to the left of it is Adj (3120m).

Out of Tamatert, you will step back onto the road – this time unpaved – and follow it slightly uphill past the last shop. At the first switchback in the road, take the footpath bearing off the corner and into the wooded hillside. Cross over a small stream and continue on a narrow dirt track through the pine trees. Looking

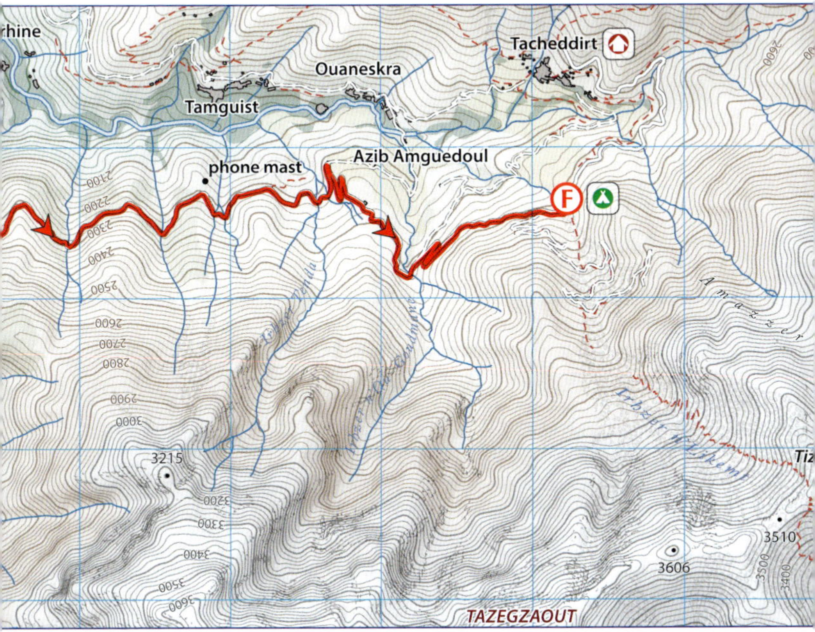

back, you can still see the distant peak of Adj beyond Imlil and the north summit of Aguelzim peeking out to its left.

The path pops out on a short section of road again then heads back into the trees. The red-and-white-striped pylon up ahead is a mobile phone mast that sits at the top of the pass you are climbing. Climb up the final slightly rocky section to the top to reach **Tizi n'Tamatert**.

At the pass stands the huge phone mast, with a red-painted police checkpoint in front of it. Around to the right of the checkpoint is a small

Tizi n'Tamatert

café with a shaded seating area. You may see herds of goats making their way across the slopes below it, completely unphased by any steepness.

> **Tizi n'Tamatert** connects the valleys of Imlil and Tacheddirt. The peak standing above the pass, Tamalaroute, can be climbed from this side; you should be able to see the start of the path winding up its south slope. This makes a detour of approximately 4km, there and back, with 400m of ascent.

Beyond the pass, continue along the road (there is almost no traffic) as it winds in and out of the bends in the hillside, slowly descending. It may be a bit hazy, but you are looking out across the Tacheddirt valley, and the largest peak opposite is Oukaïmeden, sometimes called Jbel Attar, which becomes the Oukaïmeden ski resort in winter. Continue down the road, past another red-and-white phone mast (this is a good spot to stop for lunch).

> At 2314m, **Tacheddirt** is the highest village in Morocco. A small CAF refuge was located here for many years but it has since been dismantled. Many tales of mountain adventures in this corner of Toubkal National Park in the 1950s–80s began at this hut.

Simply follow the road into **Tacheddirt**. It is possible to cut some of the corners of the switchbacks by going slightly off-piste across the slopes. A common place to camp is at the top of the road before it turns left towards Tacheddirt, directly below the footpath to Tizi n'Likemt, but other places are possible. You could also stay overnight in the village or at the guest house you pass on the road.

Along the road to Tacheddirt

STAGE 2

Tacheddirt to Azib Likemt

Start	Tacheddirt
Finish	Azib Likemt
Duration	6–7hr
Distance	11.5km (7¼ miles)
Ascent	1250m (4100ft)
Descent	1100m (3610ft)
High point	Tizi Likemt (3516m)
Common start time	7am

Today's main objective is to get over Tizi n'Likemt, the next pass, as early in the day as possible. At 3516m it is the second-highest pass on the trek and is climbed up a long and winding path on a north-west-facing slope. Many groups will set out very early from Tacheddirt to climb as far as they can in the shade before the heat of the day. Ideally, you want to be on top of the pass before noon. From there, you'll get your first panoramic view of Toubkal National Park's high mountain ridges. Beyond the pass is a long but pleasant descent down into Azib Likemt, the summer home of local nomads.

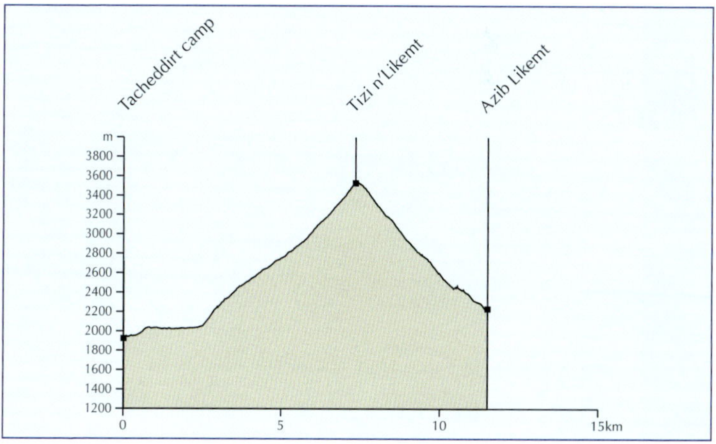

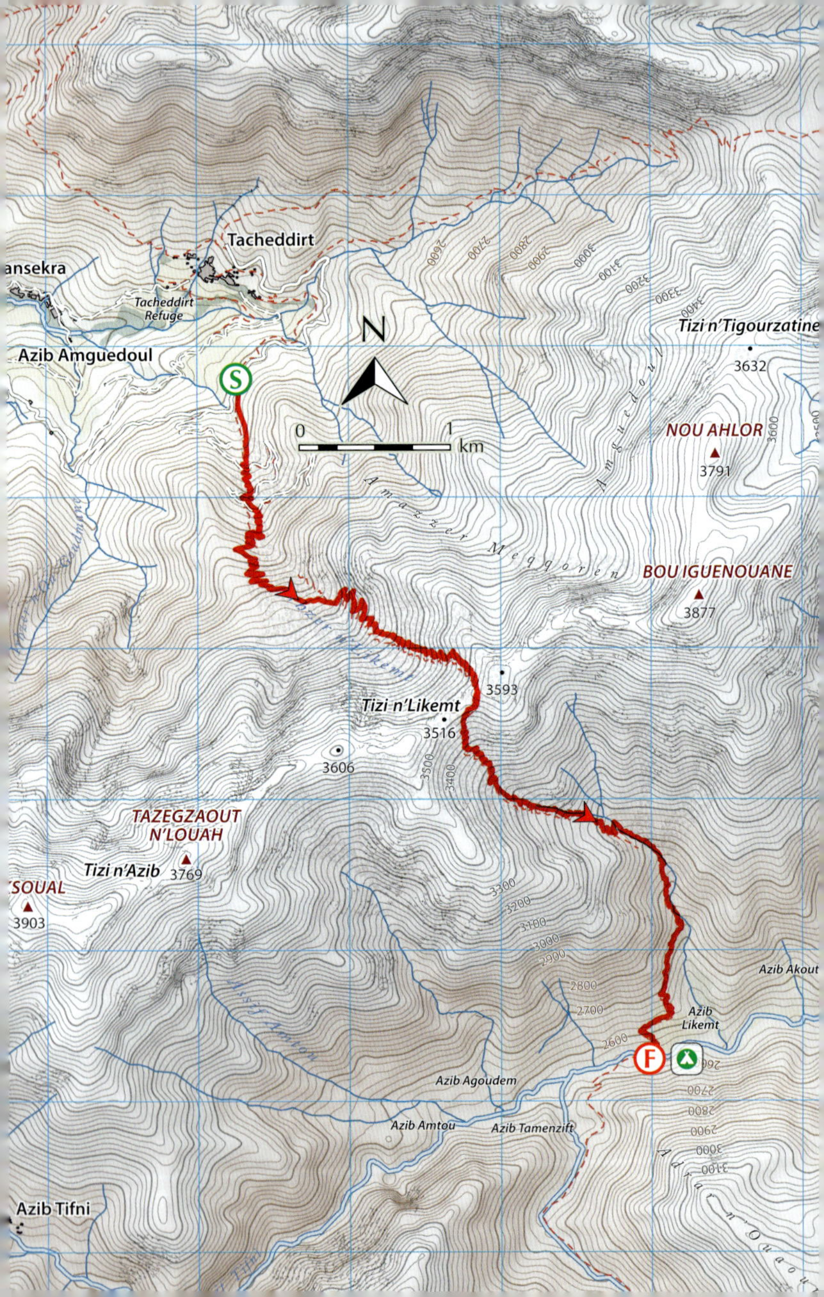

Tacheddirt
ansekra
Tacheddirt Refuge
Azib Amguedoul
N
0
1
km
Tizi n'Tigourzatine
3632
NOU AHLOR
3791
BOU IGUENOUANE
3877
Amazzer Meqqoren
Amguedoul
3593
Tizi n'Likemt
3516
3606
TAZEGZAOUT N'LOUAH
Tizi n'Azib
3769
SOUAL
3903
Azib Akout
Azib Likemt
Azib Agoudem
Azib Amtou
Azib Tamenzift
Azib Tifni
2600
2700
2800
2900
3000
3100
3200
3300
3400
3500
3600

Starting early to avoid the heat of the sun on the long ascent, cross the road and take the footpath rising up the left slope opposite the campsite. You'll start off following the course of a river valley uphill to its source. The ground underfoot is stony but not too loose. As you climb, watch the plant life change from colourful flowers to hardy, round but spiky bushes. You can almost draw a line in the ground to mark the 3000m contour.

Eventually, the path crosses to the other side of the gully and onto a little promontory that makes a good viewpoint back down the valley. You can see down over Tacheddirt on the far right and all the way across to Tamalaroute. The chairlifts of the Oukaïmeden ski resort are silhouetted by the rising sun.

Continue on the path back to the middle of the cwm, then start the many short switchbacks through the scree. This may feel long – it is! – but it is good practice for Tizi n'Ouagane, the last pass of the trip. Finally, you will step out into the **Tizi n'Likemt** pass and your first view south towards the high mountains of Toubkal National Park.

In 1888, **Joseph Thomson** climbed Tizi n'Likemt and correctly suggested that a peak in the distance was the highest in the Atlas: Toubkal.

Mules climbing out of a cloud inversion over Tacheddirt valley

The pass is a good place to stop for something to eat. There is a dilapidated hut just west of the pass and from there you have a clear view down the ridge towards Aksoual (3903m). This gives you an incredible panorama of the mountain ridge stretching from Aksoual due west through to south.

Now descend south into the bowl of the valley towards Azib Likemt. There is a path across the scree fields, though it's a little loose at the top. It swings past the bubbling crags on the left and another lighter-coloured crag on the right before reaching the stony groove of a riverbed. Here the path turns right and follows alongside the stream – you'll be able to hear it before you can see it. The landscape becomes much greener again as you descend towards the *azib*.

An **azib** is the summer home of nomads. They spend the winter in the valley villages, then the summer in the mountains with their animals. There are terraces for grazing animals and for growing many crops.

Pass to the left of the main terraces to reach the river, Assif n'Tinzer. Most people camp either on its north bank, near the huts, or on the stony south bank in the shade of Adrar n'Ouaourege.

Azib Likemt campsite

STAGE 3

Azib Likemt to Amsouzert

Start	Azib Likemt
Finish	Amsouzert
Duration	7–8hr
Distance	15.5km (9¾ miles)
Ascent	850m (2790ft)
Descent	1650m (5410ft)
High point	Tizi n'Ououraine (3103m)
Common start time	7am

After yesterday's big ascent, today's walk is fairly flat – or as the guides might say, 'mountain flat'. You'll set out from Azib Likemt following the river Assif n'Tinzer slowly uphill through gorges and a steep-sided rock valley. The route then passes through verdant mini-meadows before a short climb to the day's pass: Tizi n'Ououraine. From here you'll have clear views out towards Toubkal as you make the long descent to the village of Amsouzert for the night.

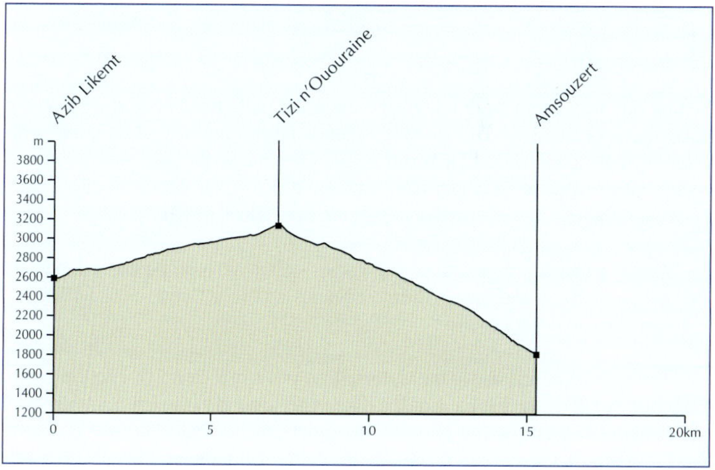

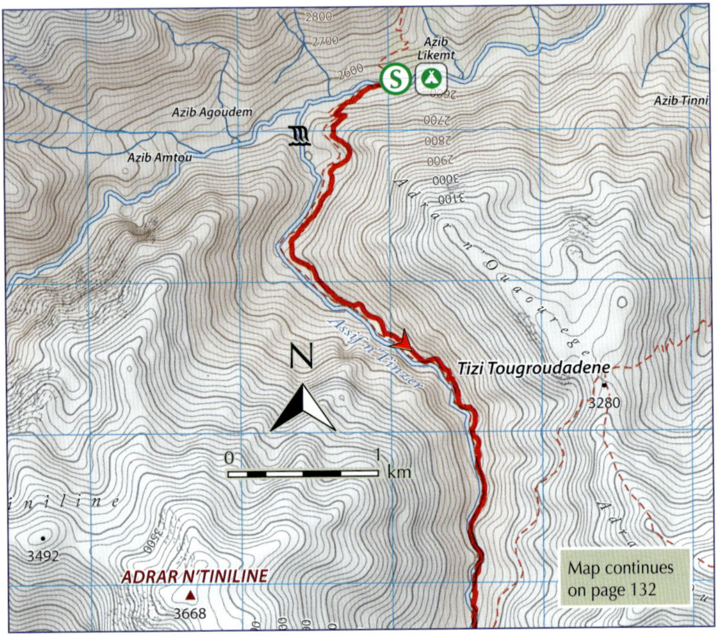

Setting out from camp fairly early, take the small path, heading due west on the south bank of the river. This quickly ascends up the north-west flank of Adrar n'Ouaourege, to follow **Assif n'Tinzer** uphill. Over the lip the path swoops around to the left across a scree slope, with walls built out of the stones on either side. Looking right, you can see the gorge that the river falls through.

> **Assif n'Tizner** is a river with several gorges – although most people will not see the ones you are passing. The most famous is Kissaria Gorge, much further east along the river's course.

The path takes you above the **waterfall**, so you can look down into the gorge. Continue uphill on the left bank as the river bears around to the left. You might see more mountain goats as you pass another much smaller azib. Above you are the flanks of Adrar n'Ouaourege to the left and Adrar n'Tiniline on the right. The valley has steep, rocky sides and you feel like you are walking up a canyon. Golden morning light reflects on the surface of the river.

Hiking through the gorge

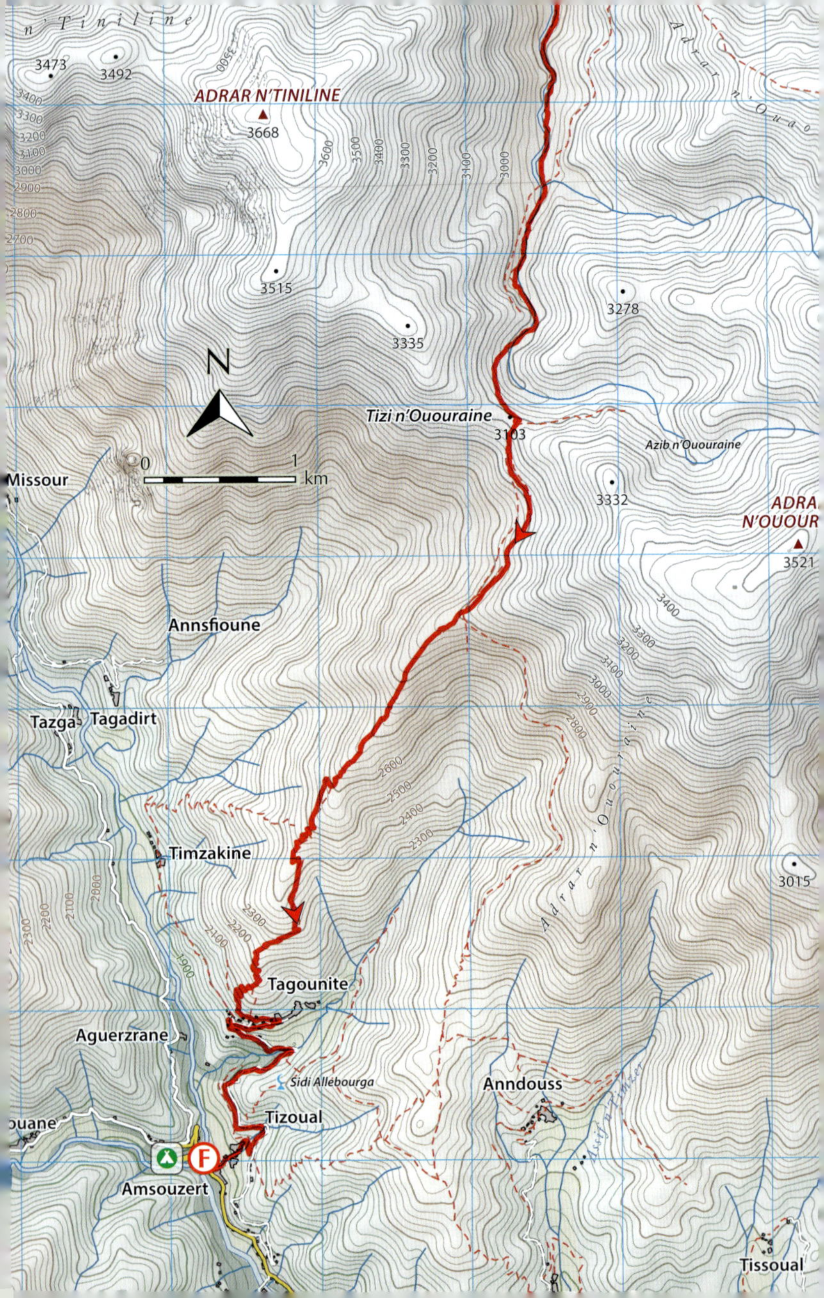

ADRAR N'TINILINE
3668
3473
3492
3515
3335
3278
Tizi n'Ououraine
3103
Azib n'Ououraine
3332
ADRAR N'OUOUR
3521
3015
N
0
1
km
Missour
Annsfioune
Tazga
Tagadirt
Timzakine
Tagounite
Aguerzrane
Sidi Allébourga
Anndouss
Tizoual
Amsouzert
Tissoual
F

As the valley opens out, walk through a pleasant green corridor of grass and flowers beside the river. Through the valley that opens up to the left, you can see Tizi n'Dern, which leads to Jbel Iferouane (4001m).

The path swaps banks a few times as the river meanders. Continue upriver until you pass through a final narrow gorge. Beyond, you'll see a path curving up a scree slope to the right. Take this path up to today's pass, **Tizi n'Ououraine**. It has a huge view. The red-tinged ridgelines are your first proper view of Toubkal. The near ridge from left to right is Quimeksane, Dome d'Ifni and Toubkal. The far ridge is Adrar Afilel through to Bou Ouzzal, and Lake Ifni is hiding between the ridges.

To descend, follow the swooping path across a curving scree slope. There is some exposure here as the path is narrow and rocky with a big drop to the right. As you descend, you'll see the tempting trees of valley villages surrounding Tagadirt down below. Instead, continue below a little crag and onto the top of a ridgeline. It is broad and open with a clear path. As the scree slopes of Adra n'Ououraine drop away to your left, the view opens up to the Anti-Atlas and Jbel Sirwa. Continue downhill between the somewhat otherworldly landscape of round bushes, drinking in the view on the slow descent to **Tagounite**.

You'll pop out into the back of the village (this last section of the path is not good). Pass through the streets between brightly painted – if somewhat precariously built – houses to meet the road. You may attract some attention as you pass through. Once down on the main valley road, follow its winding course, enjoying the shade of the walnut trees, down to **Amsouzert**.

Descent path with the Anti-Atlas in the distance

STAGE 4

Amsouzert to Lake Ifni

Start	Amsouzert
Finish	Lake Ifni
Duration	5hr
Distance	9.5km (6 miles)
Ascent	1000m (3280ft)
Descent	450m (1480ft)
High point	Viewpoint above Lake Ifni (approx 2400m)
Common start time	8.30am

Today is the shortest day of the Circuit. You'll climb steadily out of the Amsouzert valley along the road and up to Tirhaltine, the highest village of the valley. As the road ends, continue uphill along the winding track to the viewpoint above Lake Ifni: a deep blue freshwater lake surrounded by giant heaps of mountain rubble and a boulder 'beach'. It is the only lake in Toubkal National Park. From the viewpoint and small café, there is a short descent and traverse around the lake to make camp on the stony plains behind it.

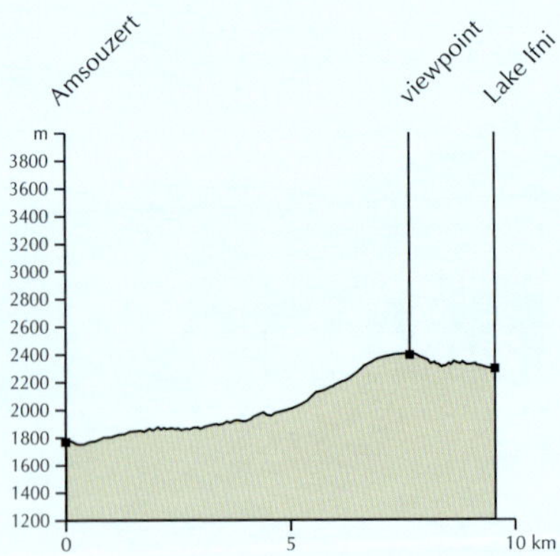

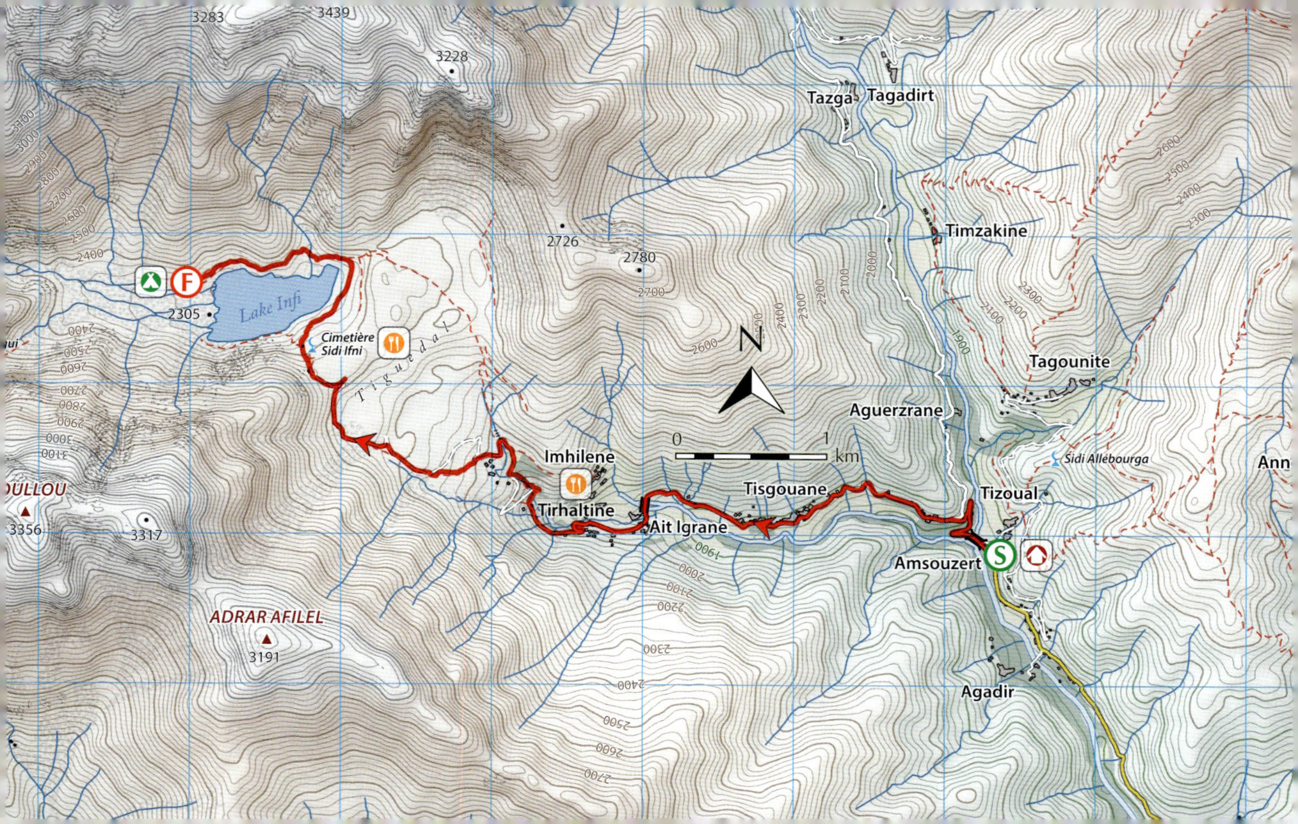

3283
3439
3228
Tazga
Tagadirt
Timzakine
2726
2780
Lake Infi
2305
Cimetière Sidi Ifni
Tigueddal
Tagounite
Aguerzrane
0
1
km
N
Imhilene
Tirhaltine
Ait Igrane
Tisgouane
Sidi Allébourga
Tizoual
Amsouzert
Agadir
ADRAR AFILEL
3191
3356
3317

From your accommodation, find the main road that runs along the bottom of the valley, parallel to the river. Follow it uphill, crossing the river at the **bridge** and winding up switchbacks until you are standing at a junction on the south-facing hillside, looking back down over Amsouzert. Take the westerly road and wander up through quiet villages. The view to the left looks steeply over the valley bottom and across to Adrar Afilel and Doullou. At the end of the road, in **Tirhaltine**, take advantage of the small café for refreshments and a break in the shade.

The next stage is a climb to today's high point, the viewpoint out over Lake Ifni. The landscape is strange and feels like a wasteland – as though a whole heap of rocks has been piled up to guard the lake from the valley. A main track zigzags in broad sweeps up to the top. You can also cut the corners via steps and small footpaths for a more direct but steeper route. Halfway up, a small hut provides some welcome shade.

The main footpath continues through the gap but it is well worth the extra 5min up to the viewpoint for a clear view out to Lake Ifni: a huge turquoise blue lake crowned by mountain peaks. When done, descend back to the main path, past a small café, and proceed down into the bowl of the cwm. The path swoops around the north side of the lake, through some interesting crags, and down to the stony shores of the lake. You'll camp further back on the plain. Enjoy the afternoon off in preparation for the long day ahead tomorrow.

Lake Ifni, sometimes Lac d'Ifni, is the only lake in Toubkal National Park. At about 2500m above sea level, it is the highest lake in Morocco and has no visible inflow of rivers. If you are going to swim in it, stay close to the edge. There are strong currents in the middle that people have become trapped in.

The high path around the side of Lake Ifni

STAGE 5

Lake Ifni to Toubkal Base Camp

Start	Lake Ifni
Finish	Toubkal Base Camp
Duration	7–8hr (5hr to the pass)
Distance	9km (5½ miles)
Ascent	1550m (5090ft)
Descent	700m (2300ft)
High point	Tizi n'Ouanoums (3658m)
Common start time	5.30–6am

This is the last day before Toubkal, and today's hike is a big one that climbs over Tizi n'Ouanoums, which, at 3658m, is the highest pass of the trek. You'll probably start very early, walking in the moonlight with a galaxy of stars overhead until the sunrise breaks into the sky behind you. The route crosses the plains behind Lake Ifni and up into a rocky gorge that gets steeper and steeper until it reaches the narrow gap of Tizi n'Ouanoums. The path is well maintained and fit for mules, so expect a lot of switchbacks as you climb. The view behind, out towards Jbel Sirwa and the Anti-Atlas just gets better and better. From the top of the pass, you'll get a full view of Ouanoukrim and across to the main ridge of 4000ers opposite Toubkal. Then, you'll descend into the wide valley down to the Toubkal refuges looking very welcoming in the distance.

Set out from your campsite along the right-hand side of the huge stony plain, heading north-west. The path is not very clear at the start and you may find yourself hopping between the larger stones. As a valley gorge opens out ahead, stay right and follow the path that leads into it. This is the valley you will be climbing up all day, but you cannot see the pass yet.

Continue on the fairly shallow ascent path into the valley, past a sheer rock wall on the left-hand side then another on the right. The path crosses to the left-hand side of the valley through some large boulders then continues to slowly wind up and up. This is a very long ascent. As the way steepens a little, you'll pass a huge boulder in the centre of the valley, some 10m^2. The path winds behind this on its left and continues up.

Another impressive, steep-sided valley joins this from the right. This area is known as Ifri n'Irouzan and seems to have some sort of mining history. You can see some pockets carved out of the steep faces on either side of the gorge.

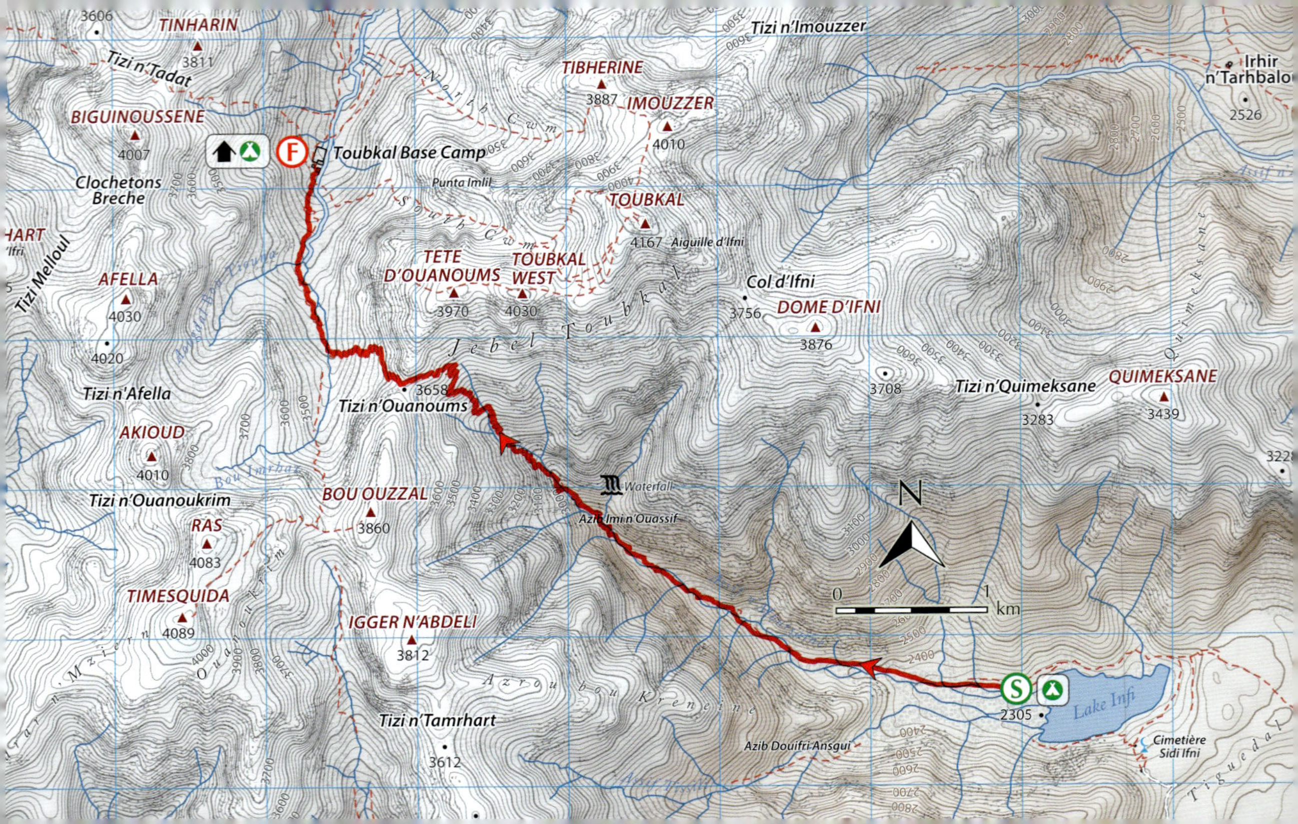
TINHARIN
3811
Tizi n'Tadat
BIGUINOUSSENE
4007
Clochetons
Breche
Tizi Mellouf
AFELLA
4030
4020
Tizi n'Afella
AKIOUD
4010
Tizi n'Ouanoukrim
RAS
4083
TIMESQUIDA
4089
Toubkal Base Camp
Punta Imlil
TETE D'OUANOUMS
3970
TOUBKAL WEST
4030
3658
Tizi n'Ouanoums
BOU OUZZAL
3860
IGGER N'ABDELI
3812
Tizi n'Tamrhart
3612
TIBHERINE
3887
IMOUZZER
4010
TOUBKAL
4167
Aiguille d'Ifni
Tizi n'Imouzzer
Col d'Ifni
3756
DOME D'IFNI
3876
Jebel Toubkal
3708
Tizi n'Quimeksane
3283
QUIMEKSANE
3439
Waterfall
Azib Imi n'Ouassif
Azib Douifri Ansgui
Lake Ifni
2305
Cimetière
Sidi Ifni
Irhir
n'Tarhbalou
2526
0
1 km
N

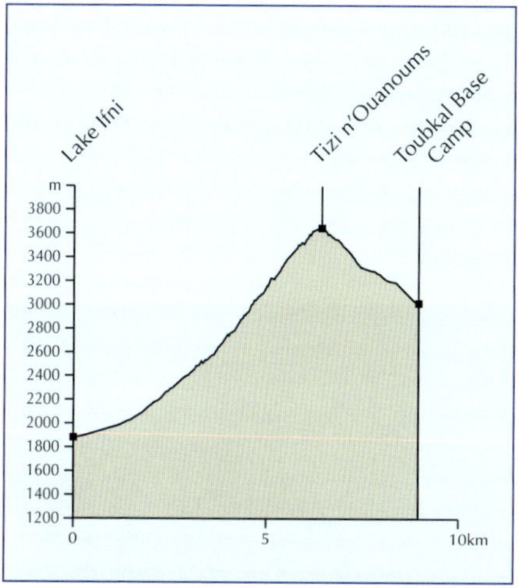

Here the path continues up to the left, passing a stream with a little waterfall. There is a small azib here too, **Azib Imi n'Ouassif**, where people sometimes camp.

Cross the river and continue upwards. The terrain gets much steeper now, but the path ascends in many tight zigzags. There is a fork in the gorges ahead of you again. Tizi n'Ouanoums is above the right side-gorge, but you still cannot see it. Follow the path as it bears into the right-hand gorge and continues uphill. The many steep switchbacks are supported by small drystone walls. Keep going up!

There are a few more open spaces where it's easy to pause for a break on the somewhat relentless uphill. You'll be in the heat of the sun by now and, as the top is still hidden, this pass can feel somewhat endless. At about 3500m, the zigzags become longer again, and the path takes you onto the bottom slopes of Toubkal West. All these crags on your right are part of the Toubkal Massif, although it's too low an angle to see the summit of Toubkal. There is a path here that cuts off up Toubkal West.

Finally, you'll turn a corner and see the notch of Tizi n'Ouanoums – very close when it finally becomes visible. The views back from the rock slab on this bend in the path are arguably better than those from the pass. So take one last look before heading over to **Tizi n'Ouanoums** and a well-deserved lunch break!

TIZI N'OUANOUMS

The highest pass on the trek, Tizi n'Ouanoums also gives you your first view into the Toubkal valley. The wide panorama of mountains contains many of the main peaks in this area: from left to right, Akioud, followed by Afella North peeking out behind Akioud's north-east ridge; the distinctive cluster of fingers is the Clochetons, leading up to Biguinoussene; and the single pinnacle of Tadat on the far right.

When you're ready, begin the pleasant descent to the Toubkal refuges. Continue on the path on long, easy zigzags down towards the valley base. As you descend, Ouanoukrim comes into view on the far left.

At the valley bottom, continue along the gently descending path towards the refuges. The valley is pleasantly verdant after the ascent gorge, and the cluster of buildings at Toubkal Base Camp are a welcome sight. As you approach, note the start of the Ikhibi Sud route on your right in case you need it for tomorrow. Toubkal itself is, illusively, still out of sight.

View of the path near the top of the pass

Descent from Tizi n'Ouanoums

STAGE 6

Toubkal Base Camp to Imlil

Start	Toubkal Base Camp
Finish	Imlil
Duration	3–4hr
Distance	10.5km (6½ miles)
Ascent	150m (490ft)
Descent	1550m (5090ft)
High point	Toubkal Base Camp (3200m)
Common start time	8am

This last day of the Toubkal Circuit is often extended to include an ascent of Toubkal first before descending all the way back to Imlil. Rather than repeat routes, flip to the earlier routes in the Summer section that describe the best routes up Toubkal. If you are staying in a refuge rather than camping, you can leave your extra luggage inside while you climb Toubkal, then repack before continuing the descent with the mules. It can be very cold in the wind on top of Toubkal, whereas the descent to Imlil is sheltered and warm.

Note that these stats are just for the descent. If you also plan to climb Toubkal, add on the extra distance, time, etc. from the particular route you are doing.

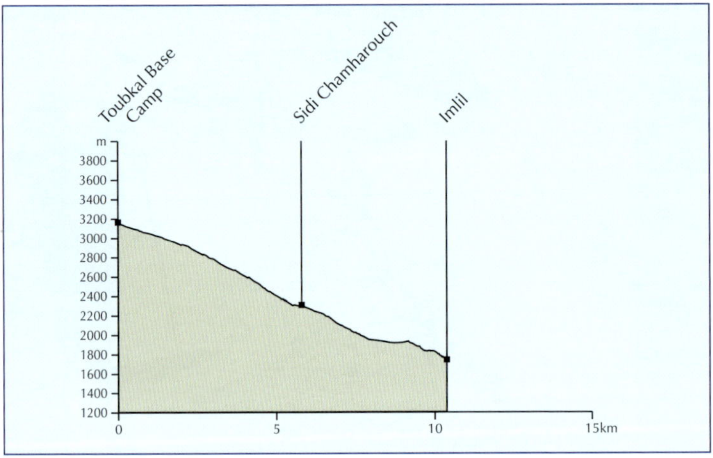

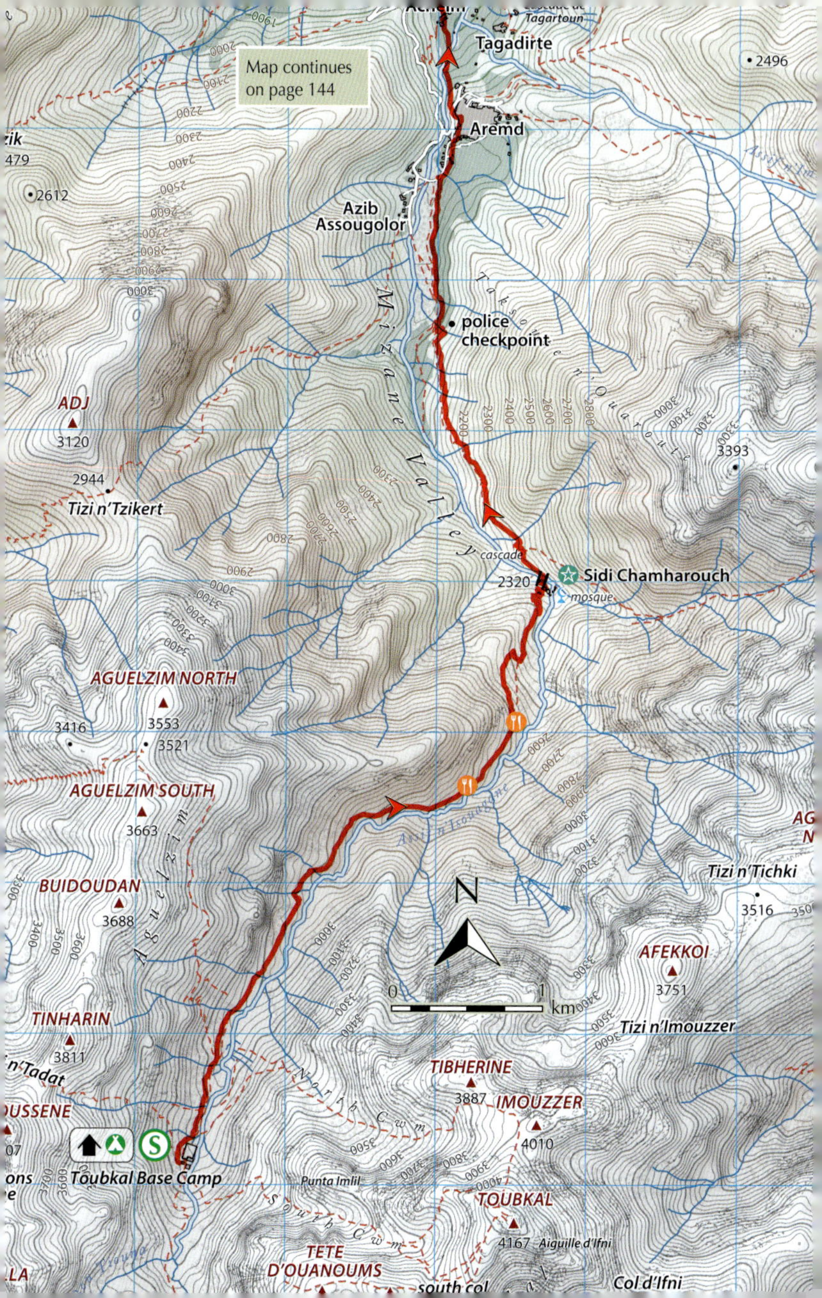
Map continues on page 144
Tagadirte
Tagartoun
Aremd
Azib Assougolor
police checkpoint
Mizane Valley
Taksoute n'Ouarour
ADJ
3120
2944
Tizi n'Tzikert
2612
2496
3393
cascade
2320
Sidi Chamharouch
mosque
AGUELZIM NORTH
3553
3416
3521
AGUELZIM SOUTH
3663
Assif n'Isougouane
Aguelzim
BUIDOUDAN
3688
Tizi n'Tichki
3516
AFEKKOI
3751
Tizi n'Imouzzer
0
1
km
TINHARIN
3811
TIBHERINE
3887
IMOUZZER
4010
North Cwm
Toubkal Base Camp
Punta Imlil
TOUBKAL
4167
Aiguille d'Ifni
South Cwm
TETE D'OUANOUMS
south col
Col d'Ifni

Descend on the long, well-made path down the left-hand slope of the valley above the river, past small cafés to **Sidi Chamharouch**. Then cross the river at the bridge there and continue downhill, past the police checkpoint, and across the alluvial plain to Aremd and Imlil. Smile knowingly at all the fresh-faced hikers you'll pass, just starting their journey towards Toubkal. For a detailed description of the route and points of interest, use the 'Imlil to Base Camp' route in reverse.

A muleteer starting down the path towards Imlil

The streets of Imlil

APPENDIX A

Language

Amazigh languages use the Tifinagh alphabet, so any words found here are transliterated into the Latin alphabet. T for Tachelhit, A for Arabic.

- hello – *salam* (A/T)
- Let's go! – *Yalla!* (A)
- no – *uhu* (T)
- no thank you – *la shukran* (A) (used as a polite refusal)
- please – *afak* (T)
- thank you – *shukran* (A) *tanmirt* (T)
- yes – *yeh* (T)

The language of the mountain landscape has influences from three successive populations: first the native Amazigh languages, then Arabic and later French. Understanding a small amount of each of these will help you engage more deeply with the places you pass through and the peaks you climb.

Note that 'Ou' at the start of a word is pronounced like a soft 'W' or 'woo' sound. In the middle of a word, it's more like 'oo' or the French '*où*'.

- adrar – *mountain* (e.g Adrar-n-Drer)
- assif – *river/stream* (e.g. Assif Tifnoute)
- azib – *generally a nomad summer settlement, or specifically a shelter for grazing animals* (e.g. Azib Likemt)
- jbel – *mountain/mount* (e.g. Jbel Toubkal)
- oued – *river or wadi*
- ras – *head/top* (e.g. Ras Ouanoukrim)
- saqia – *leat*
- sidi – *saint* (e.g. Sidi Chamharouch)
- tizi – *col/saddle/pass* (e.g. Tizi n'Ouanoums)

English to French

- north – *nord*
- south – *sud*
- east – *est*
- west – *ouest*

APPENDIX B

Glossary of mountaineering terms

Since Toubkal is used by many as an introduction to the world of mountaineering, I have included some frequently used terms that you may find in this book or hear used in the mountains.

- Arête – a narrow ridge or crest on a mountain
- Bootpack – a trail in the snow made by the compression of multiple people passing that way
- Cairn – small pile of rocks used to mark a path or a summit
- Col – a saddle or pass between two peaks: a dip in a mountain ridgeline
- Contour – to follow a line of equal height across a slope, without going up or down
- Crag – a small, often rugged, cliff face on a mountainside
- Cwm – a steep-sided hollow or bowl in the landscape near the head of a valley, pronounced 'koom' (also a *cirque* in French and a corrie in Scotland)
- Glacier – a mass of ice, formed by years of compacted snow, that moves incredibly slowly downhill
- Moraine – rock debris carried and deposited by a glacier
- Scree – piles of broken rock fragments making up a slope that can slide when stepped on
- Snowline – the point (usually a height but also a physical place) where conditions change: above is snow covered and below is not.
- Snowpack – an accumulation of snow on the ground that has compacted over time into one or several layers
- Traverse – to walk diagonally across a slope rather than directly up or down it

DOWNLOAD THE GPX FILES

All the routes in this guide are available for download from:

www.cicerone.co.uk/1199/GPX

as standard format GPX files. You should be able to load them into most online GPX systems and mobile devices, whether GPS or smartphone. You may need to convert the file into your preferred format using a conversion programme such as gpsvisualizer.com or one of the many other such websites and programmes.

When you follow this link, you will be asked for your email address and where you purchased the guidebook, and have the option to subscribe to the Cicerone e-newsletter.

LISTING OF CICERONE GUIDES

NORTH-EAST ENGLAND, YORKSHIRE DALES AND PENNINES

Cycling in the Yorkshire Dales
Great Mountain Days in the Pennines
Mountain Biking in the Yorkshire Dales
The Cleveland Way and the Yorkshire Wolds Way
The Cleveland Way Map Booklet
The North York Moors
Trail and Fell Running in the Yorkshire Dales
Walking in County Durham
Walking in Northumberland
Walking in the North Pennines
Walking in the Yorkshire Dales:
North and East
South and West
Walking St Cuthbert's Way
Walking St Oswald's Way and Northumberland Coast Path

DERBYSHIRE, PEAK DISTRICT AND MIDLANDS

Cycling in the Peak District
Dark Peak Walks
Scrambles in the Dark Peak
Walking in Derbyshire
Walking in the Peak District -
White Peak East
White Peak West

WALES AND WELSH BORDERS

Cycle Touring in Wales
Cycling Lon Las Cymru
Great Mountain Days in Snowdonia
Hillwalking in Shropshire
Mountain Walking in Snowdonia
Offa's Dyke Path
Offa's Dyke Map Booklet
Scrambles in Snowdonia
Snowdonia: 30 Low-level and Easy Walks — North, South
The Cambrian Way
The Pembrokeshire Coast Path
The Pembrokeshire Coast Path Map Booklet
The Snowdonia Way
The Wye Valley Walk
Walking Glyndwr's Way
Walking in Carmarthenshire
Walking in Pembrokeshire
Walking in the Brecon Beacons
Walking in the Wye Valley
Walking on Gower
Walking the Severn Way
Walking the Shropshire Way
Walking the Wales Coast Path

SOUTHERN ENGLAND

20 Classic Sportive Rides
in South East England
in South West England
Cycling in the Cotswolds
Mountain Biking on the North Downs
Mountain Biking on the South Downs
The North Downs Way
The North Downs Way Map Booklet
The South Downs Way
The South Downs Way Map Booklet
The Cotswold Way
The Cotswold Way Map Booklet
The Ridgeway National Trail
The Ridgeway Map Booklet
The Thames Path
The Thames Path Map Booklet
The Two Moors Way
Two Moors Way Map Booklet
Walking the South West Coast Path
South West Coast Path Map Booklet
Vol 1: Minehead to St Ives
Vol 2: St Ives to Plymouth
Vol 2: St Ives to Plymouth
Vol 3: Plymouth to Poole
Suffolk Coast and Heath Walks
The Kennet and Avon Canal
The Lea Valley Walk
The Peddars Way and Norfolk Coast Path
The Pilgrims' Way
Walking Hampshire's Test Way
Walking in Essex
Walking in Kent
Walking in London
Walking in Norfolk
Walking in the Chilterns
Walking in the Cotswolds
Walking in the Isles of Scilly
Walking in the New Forest
Walking in the North Wessex Downs
Walking on Dartmoor
Walking on Guernsey
Walking on Jersey
Walking on the Isle of Wight
Walking the Dartmoor Way
Walking the Jurassic Coast
Walking the Sarsen Way
Walks in the South Downs National Park

ALPS CROSS-BORDER ROUTES

100 Hut Walks in the Alps
Alpine Ski Mountaineering Vol 1 — Western Alps
The Karnischer Hohenweg
The Tour of the Bernina
Trail Running — Chamonix and the Mont Blanc region
Trekking Chamonix to Zermatt
Trekking in the Alps
Trekking in the Silvretta and Ratikon Alps
Trekking Munich to Venice
Trekking the Tour du Mont Blanc
Tour du Mont Blanc Map Booklet
Walking in the Alps

FRANCE, BELGIUM, AND LUXEMBOURG

Camino de Santiago — Via Podiensis
Chamonix Mountain Adventures
Cycling London to Paris
Cycling the Canal de la Garonne
Cycling the Canal du Midi
Mont Blanc Walks
Mountain Adventures in the Maurienne
Short Treks on Corsica
The GR5 Trail
The GR5 Trail —
Vosges and Jura
Benelux and Lorraine
The Moselle Cycle Route
Trekking in the Vanoise
Trekking the Cathar Way
Trekking the GR10
Trekking the GR20 Corsica
Trekking the Robert Louis Stevenson Trail
Via Ferratas of the French Alps
Walking in Provence — East
Walking in Provence — West
Walking in the Auvergne
Walking in the Brianconnais
Walking in the Dordogne
Walking in the Haute Savoie: North
Walking in the Haute Savoie: South
Walking on Corsica
Walking the Brittany Coast Path
Walking in the Ardennes

PYRENEES AND FRANCE/SPAIN CROSS-BORDER ROUTES

Shorter Treks in the Pyrenees
The Pyrenean Haute Route
The Pyrenees
Trekking the Cami dels Bons Homes
Trekking the GR11 Trail
Walks and Climbs in the Pyrenees

SPAIN AND PORTUGAL

Camino de Santiago: Camino Frances
Coastal Walks in Andalucia
Costa Blanca Mountain Adventures
Cycling the Camino de Santiago
Mountain Walking in Mallorca
Mountain Walking in Southern Catalunya
Spain's Sendero Historico: The GR1
The Andalucian Coast to Coast Walk
The Camino del Norte and Camino Primitivo
The Camino Ingles and Ruta do Mar
The Mountains Around Nerja
The Mountains of Ronda and Grazalema
The Sierras of Extremadura
Trekking in Mallorca
Trekking in the Canary Islands
Trekking the GR7 in Andalucia
Walking and Trekking in the Sierra Nevada
Walking in Andalucia
Walking in Catalunya —
Barcelona
Girona Pyrenees
Walking in the Picos de Europa
Walking La Via de la Plata and Camino Sanabres
Walking on Gran Canaria
Walking on La Gomera and El Hierro

Walking on La Palma
Walking on Lanzarote and Fuerteventura
Walking on Tenerife
Walking on the Costa Blanca
Walking the Camino dos Faros
Portugal's Rota Vicentina
The Camino Portugues
Walking in Portugal
Walking in the Algarve
Walking on Madeira
Walking on the Azores

SWITZERLAND

Switzerland's Jura Crest Trail
The Swiss Alps
Tour of the Jungfrau Region
Trekking the Swiss Via Alpina
Walking in Arolla and Zinal
Walking in the Bernese Oberland — Jungfrau region
Walking in the Engadine — Switzerland
Walking in Ticino
Walking in Zermatt and Saas-Fee

GERMANY

Hiking and Cycling in the Black Forest
The Danube Cycleway Vol 1
The Rhine Cycle Route
The Westweg
Walking in the Bavarian Alps

POLAND, SLOVAKIA, ROMANIA, HUNGARY AND BULGARIA

The Danube Cycleway Vol 2
The High Tatras
The Mountains of Romania

SCANDINAVIA, ICELAND AND GREENLAND

Hiking in Norway —
North
South
Trekking the Kungsleden
Trekking in Greenland — The Arctic Circle Trail
Walking and Trekking in Iceland

SLOVENIA, CROATIA, SERBIA, MONTENEGRO AND ALBANIA

Hiking Slovenia's Juliana Trail
Mountain Biking in Slovenia
The Islands of Croatia
The Julian Alps of Slovenia
The Mountains of Montenegro
The Peaks of the Balkans Trail
The Peaks of the Balkans Trail
The Slovene Mountain Trail
Walking in Slovenia: The Karavanke
Walks and Treks in Croatia

ITALY

Alta Via
1 — Trekking in the Dolomites
2 — Trekking in the Dolomites
Day Walks in the Dolomites
Italy's Grande Traversata delle Alpi
Italy's Sibillini National Park
Ski Touring and Snowshoeing in the Dolomites
The Way of St Francis: Via di Francesco
Trekking Gran Paradiso: Alta Via 2
Trekking in the Apennines
Trekking the Giants' Trail: Alta Via 1 through the Italian Pennine Alps
Via Ferratas of the Italian Dolomites:
Vol 1
Vol 2
Walking in Abruzzo
Walking in Italy's Cinque Terre
Walking in Italy's Stelvio National Park
Walking in Sicily
Walking in the Aosta Valley
Walking in the Dolomites
Walking in Tuscany
Walking in Umbria
Walking Lake Como and Maggiore
Walking Lake Garda and Iseo
Walking on the Amalfi Coast
Walking the Via Francigena Pilgrim Route
Part 1
Part 2
Part 3
Part 4
Walks and Treks in the Maritime Alps

IRELAND

The Wild Atlantic Way and Western Ireland
Walking the Kerry Way
Walking the Wicklow Way

EUROPEAN CYCLING

Cycling the Route des Grandes Alpes
Cycling the Ruta Via de la Plata
The Elbe Cycle Route
The River Loire Cycle Route
The River Rhone Cycle Route

INTERNATIONAL CHALLENGES, COLLECTIONS AND ACTIVITIES

Europe's High Points
Pocket First Aid and Wilderness Medicine

AUSTRIA

Innsbruck Mountain Adventures
Trekking Austria's Adlerweg
Trekking in Austria's Hohe Tauern
Trekking in Austria's Stubai Alps
Trekking in Austria's Zillertal Alps
Walking in Austria
Walking in the Salzkammergut: the Austrian Lake District

MEDITERRANEAN

The High Mountains of Crete
Trekking in Greece
Walking and Trekking in Zagori
Walking and Trekking on Corfu
Walking on the Greek Islands — the Cyclades
Walking in Cyprus
Walking on Malta

HIMALAYA

8000 metres
Everest: A Trekker's Guide
Trekking in the Karakoram

NORTH AMERICA

Hiking and Cycling the California Missions Trail
Hiking the Pacific Crest Trail
The John Muir Trail

SOUTH AMERICA

Aconcagua and the Southern Andes
Hiking and Biking Peru's Inca Trails
Trekking in Torres del Paine

AFRICA

Climbing Toubkal
Kilimanjaro
Walking in the Drakensberg
Walks and Scrambles in the Moroccan Anti-Atlas

NEW ZEALANDAND AND AUSTRALIA

Hiking the Overland Track

CHINA, JAPAN AND ASIA

Annapurna
Hiking and Trekking in the Japan Alps and Mount Fuji
Hiking in Hong Kong
Japan's Kumano Kodo Pilgrimage
Japan's Kumano Kodo Pilgrimage
Trekking in Bhutan
Trekking in Ladakh
Trekking in Tajikistan
Trekking in the Himalaya

TECHNIQUES

Fastpacking
The Mountain Hut Book

MINI GUIDES

Alpine Flowers
Navigation

MOUNTAIN LITERATURE

A Walk in the Clouds
Abode of the Gods
Fifty Years of Adventure
The Pennine Way — the Path, the People, the Journey
Unjustifiable Risk?